Franju

RAYMOND DURGNAT

UNIVERSITY OF CALIFORNIA PRESS

Produced by Design Yearbook Limited for Movie Magazine Limited, 21 Ivor Place, London, N.W.1.

Published in the United States and Canada by the University of California Press, Berkeley 94720.

Text set by Gloucester Typesetting Company Limited, 9 Market Parade, Gloucester.

Printed by Compton Printing Limited, Pembroke Road, Stocklake, Aylesbury, Bucks.

Bound by William Brendon and Son Limited, Tiptree, Essex.

© Movie Magazine Limited 1967.

Printed in England.

Library of Congress Catalog Card No 68-31139

First American edition 1968

Brief passages in the text are adapted from the article on Georges Franju in the author's Nouvelle Vague—The First Decade (Motion Publications, 1963).

Stills by courtesy of National Film Archive, Michel Caen, Forces et Voix de la France, Procinex, Comptoir Français du Film, Filmel, Contemporary, Gala, Miracle, M.G.M., Cross Channel, Amanda.

Contents

THE ARTIST

The Craftsman 7

The Seer and the Scene 8

Bureaucrats and Saboteurs 9

Voyage to the End of the Night 14

Visions and Revisions 18

A Cool Expressionism 24

The Surrealism of Science 27

Love that Brute 30

THE FILMS

Le Métro 32
Le Sang des Bêtes

En Passant par la Lorraine 43

Hôtel des Invalides 47

Le Grand Méliès 50
Monsieur et Madame Curie

Les Poussières 55
Navigation Marchande

A Propos d'une Rivière 56
Mon Chien

Le Théâtre National Populaire 59
Sur le Pont d'Avignon

Notre Dame, Cathédrale de
Paris 62

La Première Nuit 63

La Tête contre les Murs 68

Les Yeux sans Visage 78

Pleins Feux sur l'Assassin 86

Thérèse Desqueyroux 91

Judex 105

Thomas l'Imposteur 124

Les Rideaux Blancs 137

FILMOGRAPHY 139
BIBLIOGRAPHY 144

The Artist

Georges Franju is sometimes described as a New Wave director. Depending on one's definitions of the New Wave, this may be fair enough; he made what is in effect a first short film a year after Resnais' *Van Gogh*, and his first feature at the same time as *Hiroshima Mon Amour*.

In every other respect however he is a film-maker of an older generation. He was born on April 12th 1912 at Fougères, Brittany. He describes his formal education as 'summary and primary'; 'they gave me the Certificate of Primary Studies out of kindness, because I had a twin brother who worked well and you should never separate twins.' However, at the age of fifteen, he lay under the trees of the Bois de Vincennes, reading 'Fantomas' (the French pulp thriller whose utterly ruthless villain was taken, by the Surrealists and most of his fans, as the hero), and the works of Sade and Freud. 'I worked for a few months in an insurance company which I quit to nail up packing cases in a noodle merchant's. To save face I told my parents I was their cashier.' (Packing case = *caisse*; Cashier = *caissier*.) His military service was spent in Algeria, and is said to be almost his only trip outside metropolitan France. After his demobilisation in 1932, he studied theatre decor, preparing sets for the Folies Bergère and the Casino de Paris.

But his interest in cinema was a passionate one; and after he met Henri Langlois they borrowed 500 francs from Langlois' parents to finance the first programme of their *Cercle du Cinéma*. In 1934 they directed a short film together, and in 1937 they inaugurated a film magazine called CINEMAtographe, which printed contributions from Prévert, Autant-Lara, Brunius, Cavalcanti, etc., and, as good film-magazines will, lasted only two issues. In the same year they also founded the Cinémathèque Française, of which Langlois is still director. In 1938 Franju became Executive Secretary of La Fédération Internationale des Archives du Film, and from the Liberation to 1954 he was Secretary-General of L'Institut de Cinématographie Scientifique. His *Le Sang des Bêtes* inaugurated the series of documentaries which were to establish him as one of the cinema's most sensitive, and subversive, artists. In 1959 he made the first of the features which were to develop the same disturbing characteristics through fictional forms.

Franju's preferred collaborators include, notably, the cameraman Marcel Fradetal (who photographed ten of his films) and the composer Maurice Jarre (who wrote the music for eight). Franju became interested in Fradetal because he had been Rudolph Maté's associate on Dreyer's *Vampyr*, and he found Jarre after a search for a composer who would be both melodic and atonal. Like most creative personalities, Franju tends to return to the same collaborators: among them, the photographers Eugen Shuftan and Jacques Mercanton, the composers Joseph Kosma, Jean Wiener and Georges Delerue, the editor Gilbert Natot and, of course, the actors Edith Scob, Emmanuele Riva, and Pierre Brasseur.

The Craftsman

In the beginning is the vision. . . . It may surge up during a visit to a location. 'In the short film field you don't have much time to wait around for it. You can't spend too long trailing all over France or even the suburbs. You have to make up your mind quickly, to see quickly, very quickly . . . one looks, and suddenly it's all there. I knew right away that Les Invalides was full of extraordinary things . . . the same for Notre Dame. At first I thought I wouldn't find the right ingredients, after all it's a church that's nearly empty. But things all worked together as I wanted. Even if the church had been full, that would have been as I wanted it too. One chooses one's troubles. Even when what you foresaw doesn't happen, it's bound to work out, if you know how to see and choose your subjects and your objects.'

After the vision comes the word: 'It's in front of the typewriter that you must be inspired. When you get on the set, it's too late. . . . Once the shooting script is done, everything's numbered and I don't change much . . . from then on I don't count on improvisation, or rather I do count on being buggered about. . . . There are always difficulties in natural decor because you can never foresee everything. There's wind blowing, or people passing. The fireplace is on the left when you thought it was on the right. Just where you need a door, you get a staircase. . . . What's so fascinating about locations is turning the obstacles to your advantage and getting an extra something out of them. . . . You have to set up emergency solutions, or not so much set them up as sense them.'

But what can be controlled, is. As his regular composer, Maurice Jarre, remarked: 'Franju . . . has an extraordinary ear and a feeling for things, he has a sort of sixth sense which tells him just where the music ought to be. . . .' And a creator must watch over every detail of his creation: 'I never quit a film until the release print is finished—never. You can't abandon a film, everything is important.' Not that a sober obsession with nuances leads to an aesthetic cult of ornamentation or a romantic indulgence in virtuosity: 'To centre on a motor-car, fly over the decor, pass through Nogent-Sur-Marne on your way to Nogent-le-Rotrou, and end up in the Rue des Elysées on a close-up of an ashtray, is a nice job for an acrobat but doesn't attract me in the least.'

The Seer and the Scene

Franju's style has to be felt in depth. Too rapidly frisked for its meanings, it may seem lyrical rather than analytical, atmospheric rather than intellectual, hallucinatory rather than argued. But the lyrical and the analytical may imply each other. A mood, after all, is a matter of implications, which intuition has sensed before analysis has grasped. An atmosphere is a matter of assumptions and insinuations. And hallucination implies a theory about the world. Thus, the profoundly lyrical is also philosophical. Not that its 'meaning' is in the philosophy; its meaning is the representation of a sensibility impregnated by the experiences which also inspire the philosophy. In a sense, lyricism is synthesis whereas philosophy is analysis (which is why we doubt whether philosophy is an art-form in the sense that poetry is). Since Franju's sensitively lyrical eye has an immediate, overwhelming impact, this study will be particularly concerned with the bonding, by 'style', of sensibility and philosophy.

The quality of sullenness in the Franju atmosphere can easily be mistaken for inarticulacy. His sense of lonely humans against industrial walls may call to mind a less nostalgic, in fact a brutal and saturnine equivalent of

L. S. Lowry, as much a recluse from the intellectual world. His vision has the monolithic quality often associated with the Primitive. He seems more seer than analyst. Yet he is unusually analytical and lucid about his own artistic procedures and results; and if we cite his own comments on his films, it is because he is frequently their acutest critic.

Since poets so often fear the corrosive effect of self-consciousness on their inspiration, it is possible that Franju's curious blend of objectivity and passion about his work results from the fact that the sources of his vision are hermetically sealed against interference from outside, that it doesn't mind what the conscious layers of his mind are up to, that Franju, like a medium, knows exactly how to go into a trance, and can talk common-sensically throughout it, but, by all possible tests, is in a trance.

The precondition of such 'availability' is often an obsessional pressure, and, as Jean Curtelin observes, 'One thing strikes one about the man, whenever one passes a few hours in his company: that, whatever the hour of the day or night, he constantly brings the conversation round to his films. He loves reminiscing over the smallest details, he marvels at a scene shot five or six years before, evokes the joys or the difficulties which he experienced in shooting such-and-such a scene which he finds beautiful. It's not because of any egoistic presumption, but simply because he lives with his work, past and future, as intensely as others with their culture or their ambitions. Movie-making for him is a pathological necessity, explaining the minuteness with which he prepares every detail. . . .'

At the opposite extreme, an Orson Welles will confess himself bored with the run of movies, even his own, because, as a moviemaker himself, his mind's ear is constantly pricked for the sound of the clapper-board between each shot. But Franju, reliving his own

8

scenes, sees both the reality of the making and the reality within the film; both are intensely present, and intensely compatible. In Welles there is a streak of the conjurer, the showman, who baffles and amazes you by a creation which, rooted certainly in real experience, remains a 'spectacle'. Indeed the quality of spectacle, as in the paraded style of *Citizen Kane*, is part of the sense of façade and deflation which makes Welles a true poet.

But Franju is the opposite kind of artist. Every effect, every 'hallucination', edges one a little closer to a reality which one couldn't have sensed without it. Franju's films work on the mind's eye like an operation for a cataract—our culture's cataract of reassuring banalities—and his films are 'opaque' to any amount of explanation because they are transparent to a very solid reality. His stylistic effects can be analysed, but no more analysed away, than can the effects on light of cloud or fog. His style, like all styles, has its procedures, its rhetoric, its mannerisms, but, compared with the work of most noted stylists, it seems to efface itself, to turn the screen into a window. Indeed, his style is based on an intensive exploitation of just these components—*mise-en-scène* (i.e. arrangement within the shot), rhythm, lighting: in brief, visual texture—which have been seriously under-emphasised in cinema aesthetics, and under-analysed not only because of the intrinsic difficulty of verbalising cinema graphics, but because cutting, camera angles and movements are more easily isolated. Franju's style is a way of *seeing*, not of adding or adapting. It would be true, but missing the point, to say that Franju, taking meticulousness to the point of virtuosity, is able to 'transform' locations, to endow them with the expressionistic intensity usually restricted to the big studio-set (the *locus classicus* being Carné's insistence on building an entire métro-station for *Les Portes de la Nuit* so as to be able to

control every beam of light, every speck of dust, in the atmosphere). Franju seems to attain that degree of control even when exposed to the full vagaries of wind and weather. And his inspiration comes from the merger of interests which are usually allowed to become mutually exclusive. His grafting of the expressionistic and the documentary can 'take' because what he has to express is, so to speak, the dark side of the documentary moon. In his own words: 'Kafka becomes terrifying from the moment it's documentary. In documentary I work the other way round.'

Bureaucrats and Saboteurs

Before tracking-in to a close-up of Franju's documentaries, an establishing shot of the documentary field would have its uses. Because, from the mid-'30s until the mid-'50s, film criticism in English was dominated by writers who were strongly influenced by, or actively engaged in, the British documentary tradition, the impression seems to have grown up that the golden age of the documentary movement is in Britain from *Drifters* (1929) until, say, *Waters of Time* (1951). While the British school undoubtedly has its own merits, there can be little argument that, taken as a whole (and with

9

a few brave exceptions), its feeling for human experience is rudimentary in the extreme (equating sunlit smokescapes with happy workers) and that its feeling for actual social processes is smothered by a sort of bureaucratic romanticism about the functioning of the G.P.O., the Empire Marketing Board, and the sponsors of the various films.

To this tradition it is salutary to oppose all those French documentaries which show a keen concern for the individual, or carry radical overtones. Into this 'French school' it is possible to assimilate George Lacombe's *La Zone* (1928), Marcel Carné's *Nogent, Eldorado du Dimanche* (1929), Jean Grémillon's *Gardiens de Phare* (1929), Jean Epstein's *Mor Vran* (1930), Henri Storck's *Idylle à la Plage* (1931), Joris Ivens' *New Earth* and *Borinage* (1934), Henri Storck's *Les Maisons de la Misère* (1937), André Malraux's *Espoir* (1939), René Clément's *La Bataille du Rail* (1946), Georges Rouquier's *Farrebique* (1947), Yanick Bellon's *Goemons* (1948), Robert Ménégoz's *Ma Jeannette et mes Copains* (1954), Jean Rouch's *Les Maîtres Fous* (1955) and so on into Reichenbach's *Marines* (1958), Agnes Varda's *Opéra-Mouffe* (1958) and the globe-trotting *cinéma-vérité* of Jean Rouch, Chris Marker and William Klein, which (alas) has no English equivalent. Nor has the English documentary much to offer to match such pieces as Jean Painlevé's *Hippocampe* (1934), Jacques Brunius' *Violons d'Ingres* (1939), Jacques Yves-Cousteau's *Epaves* (1945) or the art films of Alain Resnais.

If the authority, and defects, of the English School arise from a schoolmasterish-bureaucratic conviction of its own superior righteousness, the spiritual richness of the French School arises from the fact that for most of its directors the distinction Documentary and Fiction was purely secondary. It's taken for granted that poems and documents are to be read between one another's lines. After all,

reality is a whole reticulation of systems, streams and strata, all interacting with those above and below and around.

The label 'documentary' implies a kind of authentication by reference to the visual surface of reality, which is unfortunate. For very little of reality exists on its visual surface. Contrary to the old saw, the camera not only often lies, it's rarely capable of seeing the truth. The abstract eludes it, as do all connections which can't be seen in physical summary from one fixed viewpoint. If editing is so vital, it's because the juxtaposition of shots is a convenient method of suggesting those realities which the camera can't see. The quickness of the cut deceives the eye; but editing is an abstract process. For the same reason, most documentaries have commentaries (or subtitles), if only to establish that dimension of generalisation without which so many documentaries would be so limited to the particular as to be almost meaningless (and, perhaps, oddly poignant). In addition to this, of course, the camera often lies, because lies are acted out, or created, before it, or because the choice of detail is deliberately rhetorical. Thus 'our side' have clear, frank, friendly faces, but the enemy soldier is scowling, and the shadows emphasise his scowl. 'Our side' are seen sunbathing in the intervals of battle, writing letters home, listening to the padre, or exhibiting manly determination, while the other side are sullen in their steel helmets, or indulging in bayonet-practice and so on. However sophisticated the eddies may be, most documentaries carry some such ideological drift. Indeed, the association between documentary and bureaucracy means that, of all film genres, it is the most heavily saturated with propaganda, whence its richly deserved reputation for the boring, pious inanity.

Recently, improvements in 16mm stock and developments in lightweight cameras have so

10

diminished the costs involved in documentary production as to cut the genre almost free from its traditional sources of finance, thus facilitating its artistic and spiritual rebirth as *cinéma-vérité*. Free Cinema can be considered a half-way house between the two, inheriting a certain ideological romanticism from the classic school, but resolved to respect the not-respectable (jazz-lovers, porters, youth) and criticize established institutions. It's significant, though, that, having completed the transformation, documentary has to be given a new name, and a French name. For, while the British school has nothing to contribute to it, *cinéma-vérité* constitutes the natural blossoming of its French seeds.

Franju's documentaries, in their formal technique and stress on processes or places rather than on individuals, relate to the old tradition. The best of them, are, for the most part, sponsored films. But if they represent that tradition at its highest pitch of aesthetic and ideological sophistication it is not entirely because of Franju's mastery of style. The conditions of film-making had to allow that mastery a certain room to manoeuvre.

Since 1945, the French documentarist has been in a rather better position than his English counterpart. The Anglo-American institution of double feature programmes leaves little room for shorts, and what niches exist are usually filled by a wretched *Look at Life*. Though documentaries occasionally creep into ordinary cinema programmes, especially in the West End, where the single-feature policy allows a little more scope, the documentary movement as a whole has always relied, not only on sponsored production, but on sponsored distribution and exhibition. You please *all* your sponsors, or you don't get shown. And what even runs the risk of displeasing won't be made.

In France, the customary single feature cinema programme accommodates documentary shorts. The tendency of a protected market to encourage the 'quota quickie' is to some extent offset by the government's *prime de qualité*, a substantial cash grant with which films of a certain artistic standard are rewarded. (If only successive British governments had preferred such a system to the wretched Eady Money, most of which now goes straight into Hollywood coffers!) The documentary is more intimately linked with the ordinary cinema programme, and it is easy to see how this checks the de-humanisation which has so constantly menaced the British tradition. And since a director like Franju is a very good bet for a *prime de qualité*, he has far more authority vis-à-vis his producers than his English counterparts.

The relation with the sponsor is profoundly different. Their absolute dependence on bureaucracy and industry means that the vast majority of British documentaries are whole-heartedly devoted to the greater glory of the Empire Marketing Board, the General Post Office, the Ministry of something or other, Shell, I.C.I., and so on. At best the documentarists could work on the system's internal contradictions, could play one sector of the establishment off against another, borrow from Peter to pay Paul. *Housing Problems* could make its passionate call for slum clearance, because it was sponsored by a Gas Company, who wanted slums demolished, so as to sell gas appliances galore for the new houses. Thus, one of the very few even mildly radical British documentaries is a fruit of vested capitalist interest! And it's no accident that it goes out of its way (stressing the killjoy caretaker in the new flats) to imply a warning against the dangers of regimentation that go with planning, i.e. Socialism. Occasionally, split-level films were possible, though the English documentarists, less radical and less ingenious than Franju, made little or no use of what possibilities existed (although *Every Day Except Christmas* and *We are the Lambeth Boys* are both commercials for Ford Trucks).

In France, however, the documentary short, even if it did little or nothing for a sponsor, or failed to please its producer, could earn a *prime de qualité* or so delight critics or audiences as to become a good box-office property. There was a multiplicity of courts of appeal, which can be played off against one another.

For the box-office is not always the villain which it is often made out to be. In itself, it is far more liberal than almost any sponsor. Not always, of course: one can't altogether blame exhibitors for virtually boycotting *Le Sang des Bêtes*, and I'm afraid that wild horses wouldn't drag me into the cinema to see it again. But it earned its substantial *prime*, it enjoyed a long career in film societies and art-houses all over the world. A multiplicity of courts of appeal can only help the nonconformist film.

Unfortunately, of course, the box office is never allowed free play. For the pressures on the film-maker originate not only from the pattern of public taste, but also from the structure of the industry, and from the consensus of trade opinion about what those patterns are. One of the tenets of this consensus is that any form of protest, of criticism, of accusation, even of regret, about any established institution or procedure, is 'controversial', and that the public, in the cinema, dislikes controversy, which upsets or depresses it. On the other hand, blanket approval of every institution or procedure is considered to be not only non-controversial, but not even propaganda. France is a little more fortunate than England, in its longer tradition of radical dissent and in the sharper conflicts in the social scene: a non-conforming attitude is less of a heresy than it seems here. Nevertheless, the limits within which the film-maker has to work are very much narrower than those of the artist in any other

field (except, in France, T.V.; in England this position is reversed).

Until very recently, the director who didn't make films under these conditions didn't make films at all. Hence Franju, like Resnais and most radical, independent directors, was condemned to operate in a clandestine way. The four main forms of subversion might be labelled the split level tactic, the counterpoint game, the oblique angle, and poetic licence. In the first, one places one's real meanings so quietly and precisely that only those who are sensitive to them will respond to them. Usually, people who would be upset by them don't see them, since they see the film in the same terms in which they see everything else. Reactions to films are sufficiently diverse for details which escape the attention of one person to flood others with delight. In the counterpoint game, one appeals to most showmen's knowledge that the spectator will quite readily grasp a point from a hint, and enjoy statements which are less obvious, or more oblique, or pleasingly restrained, or which refresh or stir his spirit by emphasising unusual aspects of the subject, or ring true by accommodating aspects which act as 'concessive clauses' to the main statement. For example, even militaristic films have to admit that war is hell. But discreet shifts of emphasis can strengthen the concessive clause until it cancels out the main clause, or becomes the main clause (or cancels out the main clause for the 'uncommitted' spectator, while becoming the main clause for the sympathetic one). The oblique angle is an unforeseen aspect of a given plot (thus a story about the bravery of the rank-and-file can be made to emphasise the ineptness or callousness of the generals). Even if a producer sees that the film has been altered, by any of these methods, he may not think revamping worth all the extra fuss and expense. In any case, producers are constantly looking for new slants on old plots, so that con-

12

formist directors not infrequently make subversive films simply because the number of possibilities is limited. Poetic licence could also be called prophetic licence or showman's licence: it is claimed when a director (or writer) has sufficient prestige, either as an artist or as a maker of box-office hits, for The System to give him leeway, or the public to reflect even upon these attitudes which it detests. All these methods of subversion are freely used by film-makers in the West and in Eastern Europe alike, not only for overtly political reasons, but because of moral pressure-groups, the trade consensus, the tastes of the audience, and various other reasons. The situation is so confused that censors often launch their most furious attacks on concessive clauses

Still: the beginning of the process in Le Sang des Bêtes.

in the work of generally conformist artists who, for one reason or another, freewheeled a little. Even books like this one don't blow the gaff. They're only one critic's opinion: critics often disagree among themselves, and every movie artist knows how forced, strained or eccentric critical exegeses can be. Hence producers are more likely to be gratified by the number of words written about Franju's movies than alarmed by what the words say about the subversive interpretations which they place on Franju's work.

These asides, brief as they are, on the strange conditions in which Franju, like so many artists, has to work, are necessary if we are to understand why Franju's movies, like Buñuel's, are so often so sly. Truth is, after all, a still, small voice, and isn't in the gilt-edged trumpetings of official rhetoric—or of the consensus.

The pressures of the system explain why Resnais and Franju have both taken care to remark that they have never offered a subject to a producer, but merely accepted, and transformed, the best of various assignments which they were offered. The scruple may smack of casuistry (if one transforms, why not initiate?). But it has its *raisons-d'être*. First, it reminds us that, however successful the films they have made, those which they might have made, if film-makers were really free, would have been much more ferocious and open. Second, it implies a healthy respect for the pitfall into which the subversive artist is likely to fall. The temptation is to offer a producer an ideal subject, and then, in the face of difficulties and pressures, steadily soften and betray it. Much better, both practically and artistically, is to take a less ideal subject, to add complexity and nuances. The first procedure plays into the hands of the consensus (a subversive subject is softened); the second raises doubts about the consensus (a safe subject becomes disturbing). The first procedure would earn the director a

14

reputation as a man who creates difficulties, and quite possibly silence him altogether; the stress on the ability to transform assignments also stresses that he is an utterly reliable craftsman who awards his producer the extra bonus of critical acclaim.

None of this implies that the films which Franju and Resnais have made are merely the ghosts of films which they might have made. Their stealthiness is part of their complexity, their sullen finesse is attuned to an age where only melodrama is allowed to challenge complacency.

Voyage to the End of the Night

Franju's lyricism, far from being an innocent spontaneity, is the natural expression of a commitment in the direct line of Vigo, Prévert and Buñuel. 'For me . . . content is a matter of the human problem . . . and that centres on certain things which I think ought to be asserted . . . among them is a hatred of the military and a hatred of priests. . . .' 'Anything said against the military and the priesthood is well said.' In his concern for the victims of the traps laid by society his left-wing anarchism is clearly visible.

Unfortunately though, left-wing and anarchist are sometimes assumed to be synonymous, and it's worth pointing out that there are also varieties of right-wing anarchism (represented in films by, notably, Frank Capra, Michael Powell and King Vidor). Moreover, the left-wing anarchist can no more escape the tragic paradoxes of political activity than anyone else, notably those involved in the great dispute between reformers over ends and means. (Do violent means inevitably corrupt one's peaceful ends, or are the ends merely conscience-titillating pipedreams unless one faces the necessity for violent means?) Franju, if a remark in a 1957 interview fairly represents his point of view, is a hawk rather than a dove. 'I'm even the opposite of an anarchist, because from the moment where what's needed is collective action, I detest everything that's individual . . . when all's said and done, loving your neighbour is all very sweet, but we have to destroy before we can rebuild. And I think we might begin, as Saint-Just recommended, by depriving the enemies of liberty of *their* liberty. And then we'll go towards liberty automatically, whether liberty of action or liberty of art.'

It is also, of course, possible to argue *both* that violent means corrupt peaceful ends *and* that the scrupulous are all but helpless. One can speak of a nihilistic anarchism, whose most notable screen representative is Jean-Luc Godard (who might be described as a humanist precipitated by despair into a nihilism which would be right-wing if it weren't rendered masochistic by its humanist reflexes). *Cahiers du Cinéma* once compared Franju to Céline, the anguished near-nihilist who hated Jews so much that he collaborated with the Nazis during the occupation. It's true that the immediate basis of their comparison was the fact that Franju's conversational style resembled Céline's prose style, in its torrential vehemence, its unabashed contradictions, and its liberal garnishing with words like '*emmerdement*' and '*con*'. But anyone familiar with *Cahiers*' gift for political confusionism will be quite sure that the political paradox was intended to carry the implication: 'opposites meet, Franju might almost be Fascist, Céline might almost be Socialist, what does it matter. . . .?' At this rate, one might as well compare Franju with Jacopetti, who also makes pessimistic documentaries involving cruelty to animals. But one of the innumerable differences is that, whereas, as Franju says, 'I'm always on the side of the victims', Jacopetti isn't on anyone's side. Since there are no sides, one might as well allow chaos to carry on; *Women of the World* even laments, discreetly, modern attempts to spare Woman the suffering which she was meant to bear.

In his emphasis on unescapable suffering, Franju's vision is a pessimistic one. But he qualifies it as an *active* pessimism, as opposed both to the passivity of the nihilists, and as opposed to the quietism of the pious. Those for whom this world is a vale of tears are predictably eager to clasp Franju to their clammy bosoms. In the Catholic review *Télé-Ciné* Madeleine Garrigou-Lagrange tries to soften Franju's riotously anticlerical and atheistic set into 'agnosticism'. And the extremely sensitive and astute Henri Agel sets, lovably, about 'saving', and betraying, Franju with the critical equivalent of the Judas kiss. Taken at face value, his comments abound in insights:

'Franju's particular quality of magic is . . . due, as with Vigo, to a fundamental feeling of malaise before life. With Franju, this malaise comes to acquire a planetary scale: it is not the human condition so much as the very essence of life which troubles him. Franju would thus be much more Hindu that Western. But he is also heir to the European tradition, in its agonised response to tragedy and death. Is not the unifying factor of the three panels of this triptych (*Le Sang des Bêtes*, *En Passant par la Lorraine*, *Hôtel des Invalides*) the shouldering of sympathy with the soul of a world (there is something it seems of Unamuno in Franju) crushed by monstrous powers? From this angle, the militarism and the bellicosity stigmatised in *Hôtel des Invalides* are no more than the precise and historically defined expression of the cosmic processes which make of every activity on the planet the activity of a torturer. The reference in *Le Sang. des Bêtes* to Baudelaire ('Je te frapperai sans colère—et sans haine comme un boucher') is no verbal play, but the indication of a strange affinity of temperament between the sado-masochism of the author of *Les Fleurs du Mal* and Franju's horrified fascination before the functioning of these murderous mechanisms.'

One can catch Agel's drift: '*either* Franju has a pathological fascination with violence, *or* his blasphemies are the cries of a St Francis of Assisi, who, in his suffering, refuses to find the good shepherd—but doubtless the good shepherd will find him.' Another implication appears: 'Since injustice is part of a cosmic process, one cannot hope to remedy it, or even comprehend it by merely human logic. Even protest is naive: one can only hope to transcend it, by taking the suffering on oneself, as Our Lord showed us by his example on the cross. When Franju shoulders his sympathy with the world's soul, is he not, unknown to himself, picking up his cross and following in the path that leads to Golgotha. . . .?' When Agel speaks of Franju's 'malaise', of cruelty 'troubling' him, of his 'Hinduism', he begins the soft-pedalling of Franju's rage in a way which makes Franju seem, at heart, another resigned, lachrymose, praying neo-Christian. The tonus of Franju's work is more accurately rendered by Franju's own qualifications to the description 'pessimist', which he accepts: 'Obviously, you have to be pessimistic. . . . Once I've

16

eliminated all the undesirable potentialities I can be sure of winning, but I have to believe in all those potentialities before I can eliminate them . . . I think that pessimism is very profitable, and that it leads . . . first to fighting . . . and then to a happy outcome.'

The pattern is that of 'revolutionary optimism', as opposed to that 'quiescent optimism' which belittles tragedy (so clouding man's vision and depriving suffering of dignity) or implies that this is more or less the best of all possible worlds (a conclusion so dismal it leads straight to the invention of Heaven). Indeed, once earthly pessimism has led to an acceptance of God, then it's back to the complacencies of 'His eye is on the sparrow', a viewpoint which is the antithesis of Franju's and whose usual applications help to explain why Franju's anticlericalism is as relentless as his antimilitarism. Priest and general are traditionally comrades-in-arms, the former preaching acquiescence in the strategies of the latter, the latter relying on the moral authority which the church is so eager to confirm.

The deep terror exhaled by Franju's films comes from the fact that no Christian, no mystic, no pantheist or even vitalist consolation is permitted to console us for the brutalities of injustice, in its extreme form (execution), being part of a cosmic process. Some of it is avoidable, but isn't avoided. But much of it is unavoidable. The avoidable should be remedied, the evil we still choose to inflict should be acknowledged, and felt, what can't be changed must still be protested against:

'Do not go gentle into that good night,
Rage, rage against the dying of the light.'

Hence the finesse of Franju's style arises, not from any soft-pedalling of rage, but from the desire to resensitize, after the hardening effect of optimism and moral cowardice. As Franju said of Clouzot's *Les Diaboliques*, 'The trouble with Clouzot is that he tries to knock the audience's head off. That's wrong; you should twist it off.' Hence, one has reservations about Ian Cameron's feeling that '*Le Sang des Bêtes* . . . certainly doesn't suggest that everything is just dandy down at the abattoir, it has no ambitions to campaign for better conditions. If Franju had aimed to do that, he would have played up the horror. . . . He treats the abattoirs as objects which fascinate him; there is nothing in the film to suggest that he finds them or their business repellent in any way. . . . Franju . . . (shows) . . . the inside of a slaughterhouse for its interest and beauty. . . . This feeling which is very far from romantic, comes through in his technique which avoids departure from eye-level shooting with normal lenses except when there is a sufficient reason. It is also detectable in his choice of subjects, necessary institutions like slaughterhouses, dog pounds, mental hospitals, and the Métro or people doing what they have to do—the Curies and even Méliès.'

One can go much of the way with this gloss. Certainly Franju's urge is to explore the processes of reality without indulging the romantic possibilities of moralising, or trying to make us all turn vegetarian, or even making us moan 'Yes, we're all guilty' like the congregation at a revivalist meeting for nonconformist liberalism. It's salutary to query whether the spectator's impulsive response to the subject-matter is necessarily the director's, and it's true enough that Franju's central concern is simply to remind us that pork chops don't grow on trees and drop on our plates when they're nicely ripe. But it's not so sure that he doesn't expect us to find even the necessary beauty terrible, or to query whether abattoirs really use every humane device possible (one remembers Brigitte Bardot, the mascot of the left, campaigning for just such a device a decade or so after the film was made). And when Franju insists that it's always the victim who interests

him, it's evident that his concern is to make us share, as he does, the outrage to the victim. As Franju explains:

'The death of the horse who seems to curtsey as he falls constitutes the first of the butchery sequences in *Le Sang des Bêtes*. The dramatic beauty of the movement was worth setting off, that is to say, being prepared.

'It's for the sake of this aesthetic realism that I chose (as commentary) . . . a slightly childish girl's voice, confidential and slightly "veiled", like the sky, to speak over these exteriors, the rigorous, beautiful and sometimes ironic commentary by Jean Painlevé. This voice is first overlaid on "amiable views" (as Méliès would have said) of the second-hand dealers' displays, and its contrast with the first image of butchery (the horse) provokes the lyrical explosion which should, of course, be accompanied by a violent shock to the startled spectator, and a surge of indignation among those who love domestic animals because they amuse them, wild beasts because they think they're tamed, and the edible animal so long, of course, as the evidence of the sacrifice doesn't spoil their appetite. . . .' The assumption that the likeliest alternative to a sort of gamp-brandishing moral indignation is blandly to admire 'the beauty of slaughterhouses and slaughter' smacks rather of the nineteenth century and of Oscar Wilde. It's understandable that a later generation of 'satirists' should continue equating protest with naivety, and a tragic sense with over-earnestness; but if these equations assert a necessary realism against liberal sentimentality, they also mask a secret despair. The paradox is that the nonconformist conscience blunts Franju's sharpness, by all but obliging the sensitive critic to overreact against it.

Indeed, the stress on eye-level shooting and on people 'doing what they have to do' all but brackets Franju with Hawks, a director whose stiff-upper-lip acquiescence in various sado-masochistic occupations has a somewhat ambivalent fascination for contemporary heirs to a sentimental culture (hence Hawks and Godard are currently principal 'cults'). It's certainly true that Franju's rage doesn't take aesthetically naive forms, nor tempt him on a search for scapegoats ('all butchers must be sadists') or to a mystificatory reformism ('If only we used more humane techniques, *then* we could forget that we kill to eat'). All this does put Franju in a very different bracket from those 'reforming' movies which (in their now slightly archaic form) put all the blame on 'the sadistic warden' or (in their more sophisticated form) put a little blame on everyone else too (the ineffectual psychiatrist, the negligent Board of Governors, the sensation-hungry journalists, the sentimental official who wasn't severe enough with the really vicious convict, the general public whose paranoia makes it impossible for the decent con to go straight, and so on), while miraculously contriving not to blame the system as a whole. If Franju can refrain from such approaches, it's because in his thinking there's a good deal of Marx and of Sade. Marx showed that even the sensitive man can function in a brutal way. As a person, he may be exceptionally kindly to those with whom he is in a face-to-face relationship; yet, in his impersonal relationships (the System), he still functions as the hard-faced capitalist of political myth. There's nothing, except lucidity, to stop one from being a villain and a good guy at one and the same time. (Once this has been grasped, a great deal of left-wing romanticism becomes totally irrelevant; one doesn't have to believe that the working-classes are the saintly classes and the upper classes thorough villains; one is freed from the massive Manichean charge present in traditional Christianity, and even in the traditional liberalism which evolved from it.) Sade's lucidity was somewhat clouded by his

hatred of the idea of God, but, even in its monstrous excess, his reversal of the enlightenment's rationalist optimism (which is the other ingredient of liberalism) breaks down that glib assumption of benevolence which remains a primary form of confusionism, by suggesting that the system is devoid of malevolence.

Visions and Revisions

The combination of anarchism, Freud, Marx and Sade must bring Franju very near a Surrealist position (indeed *La Tête contre les Murs* can be considered a cinematic equivalent of Breton's 'Essays In Simulated Madness'). Like Resnais, Franju has declared himself a blood brother of the Surrealists: 'I have always been in full agreement with the Surrealists. I have learned a great deal from them.'

As pitilessly as Aragon, he distinguishes real Surrealism (which the Surrealist group never claimed as its monopoly) from literary salon tics. 'One day, someone said to me, "I've got a Surrealist idea; we take a telephone and put it in a pot of jam." I told him: "Don't be an idiot. You might possibly put a telephone in a pot of jam by mistake, but you couldn't take a telephone out of a pot of jam and that's what's Surrealist. . . . That's when the telephone becomes as significant as a grand piano on the public highway. That's why children always remember moving house, in a special way. Because at last they *see* all the sideboards and wardrobes and knick-knacks which they saw in their home (and didn't see just because they were in their home). The object becomes itself from the moment that it's a grand piano stuck in front of an omnibus. Then the grand piano really is a grand piano, and kids always remember things like that. . . . I remember one day when I was tiny I found myself before a wardrobe with a mirror . . . I opened it and because the wardrobe was damp the inside was infested with mushrooms. . . . The sight startled me, and has probably established a certain mechanism in my sense of the bizarre. . . .'

'If the Hôtel des Invalides hadn't been situated in Paris, if the Seine didn't run alongside, I'd never have shot *Hôtel des Invalides*. If the Lorraine steelworks weren't surrounded by wheatfields, I'd never have shot *En Passant par la Lorraine*.'

The mere 'colliding' of objects can, of course, rapidly become a cliché; whether the result is poetry or platitude depends on (a) the subtlety and intensity of the objects' associations (like Lautréamont's encounter of a sewing machine and an umbrella on an operating-table), (b) the relationship between the juxtaposition and its context (which is another juxtaposition), and (c) the richness of 'style'. Any window dresser can mate sabres and seashells, telephones and jampots, etc. Its another thing to bestow upon these incongruities the richness which prevents an interpretation from depriving them of their incongruity, the internal necessity such that the reference is not just to somebody's psyche, but to a world in which we might all move. In Franju, the reference is constantly to the objective world in which we do all move, and at which our eyes unseeingly stare. Far from cutting out the real world, his vision lets it in.

No comment can better Gabriel Vialle's citation of Paul Eluard: 'There *is* another world, but it's inside this one.' Franju's style, inspired by the same spirit, is less a matter of creation than of conjuration. And his remarks about style have to be interpreted in that light. Thus he draws a rough distinction between the feature movie's predilection for subjects (stories, themes) and the short movie's predilection for objects (if we count places and processes as objects). And '. . . what really matters is to give this object a style . . . the style must be there whatever the object. Whether a painter does an apple or a cathedral, we recognise his style, and there's no reason why the same principle shouldn't apply to a film director.' Left at that, style might seem something external to the objective world, a subjective ghost in the communal machine. But this impression is dissipated by Franju's comparison between two sorts of mind's eye. The layman's eye is, so to speak, 'of very short focus, . . . he has a wide field of vision, he sees everything . . . and nothing in particular. . . . But the film-maker's mind's eye must be very long focus . . . must see far and in depth, right into the object. . . . He isolates the object and gives it its pure form . . . the more the object is surrounded, the falser it is . . . it's pulled out of its own shape by all that surrounds it. . . .'

Thus the 'collision' of objects becomes only one method of isolating them, of divesting them from that cluster of associations which prevents us from seeing them in themselves. 'To take an example from *Le Sang des Bêtes*. Generally when you see a barge it's in water. But if the barge is going through a field, and you can't see the water, it becomes startling, but it really is a barge, with its characteristic movement, and it looks thoroughly unreal.' In general: 'I'm led in my films to give documentary reality the appearance of fiction.' The same search for the familiar-strange underlies his quest, in the studio, to 'bring alive . . . that little sound that's so very familiar even though you don't actually hear it very often. . . .'

But this endowment of the real with artificiality is the opposite of ornamental enrichment. 'The camera angle is a choice, the lighting is a choice, the subject is a choice, everything is a choice, and the result of all your choices is that the object acquires its strangeness (*l'insolite*). It's the bad combination, it's the wrong synthesis, constantly made by the eye as it looks around, which stops us seeing everything as strange. In fact people with fever go on to have hallucinations, partly because really they're seeing . . . what's there to be seen, if you take the trouble. . . .' This approach to perception and emotions parallels Ehrenzweig's explorations of the interaction between depth and *Gestalt* psychology. If our memories didn't conventionalise our perceptions, everything would be 'magic', both fresh and frightening, at last we would *see*, as perhaps those under certain hallucinogenic drugs really see, because certain emotional defences, and the preconscious processes bound up with them, have been weakened, leaving the subject free to see the outside world in a novel and vivid way. Whether the subject finds himself in heaven or hell depends on internal factors: which drug he's taken, which emotions he's been repressing, so that, though he sees the world more clearly, he is, ironically, apt to become spiritually detached from it. But in Franju, the pure 'seeing' is linked to the processes of reality; what is lost is interior convention, not the outside world.

For, at the same moment that it is 'isolated', the object is related to those aspects of reality against which our complacency and optimism are defences. As one sees, one's heart sinks. This new context isn't a rhetorical trick. For the world is sadder than we choose to think, just as there is more poetry in it than we dare find. This is the poetry which, as we shall see, Franju,

like the Surrealists, believes is the countervailing power to tragedy, but it is one of which few of us are sufficiently pessimistic to avail ourselves. So we remain trapped in the optimistic. Franju's positivity is not asserted by any switch of style so much as by certain symbols, or symbol-personalities, the style remaining, if not bleak, at least elegiac. The sad isolation of objects creates a world-mood in which hope and joy, very quietly, almost occultly, survive.

Franju doesn't add a lyrically tragic note to the ordinary; he removes the ordinary to reveal the tragic. His style is subtractive, rather than additive. Thus he makes us look deeply at what, ordinarily, we merely sense, before we rapidly shift our attention to something more congenial. His opening shots of Paris monuments and tourist-traps don't try to persuade us that Paris is gay, poetic, or bitter-sweet, or how romantic it is that these worn steps have known the slow steps of devout worshippers down the centuries, or that, in this unassuming street, ordinary people live out the wonder of their modest existence, or that this monument is particularly worthy of our interest. So we can feel what we often feel before, for example, St Paul's Cathedral. Strip it of its romance, and it is inside as dark and empty as a railway terminus where the trains have ceased to run. We might be inside the rotted-out carcass of an ideological whale. Westminster Abbey abounds in decaying battle-honours evoking spiders-webs; the vast majority of its monuments are pathetically ugly and inappropriate. Franju's bleak climate withers the conventional associations which, implanted by the rhetoric of schoolroom, church, guidebook and university, usually spring up like gaudy weeds and choke the seed of matter-of-factness.

Not that Franju's movies deprive us of relevant information or tourist interest; but instead of letting it lure us into a state of edified respect, he guides us, instead, around the object as

20

object. This subjective process anticipates the *nouveau roman* (which is often described as a school of *le regard*), peeling the skins off reality's onion to reveal its core as a void. And a comparison between Franju and Robbe-Grillet is illuminating; Robbe-Grillet, too, shows a triple-barrelled interest in sheer documentation (the novels), in 'hallucinationism' (*L'Immortelle*) and in 'Surrealist' fantasy (*Marienbad*).

Robbe-Grillet's paraded concern with impartial descriptions of objective reality has successfully distracted critical attention from the extremely partial incompleteness of his descriptions. The no-nonsense, scientific air of his attacks on anthropomorphism have appealed to the secret masochism of the art world when confronted with that *other* culture which is the real determinant of the Western imagination, and therefore, though partly by reaction, of its own. (It's typical of its own confusions that, not daring to attack technological utilitarianism, it attacks scientific culture instead.) Not only does Robbe-Grillet appear as the puritanical-scientific chastiser of literary fancies, but his conspicuous caution about describing subjective realities creates an atmosphere of delicate scrupulousness which recalls the hesitations and revisions of Henry James. However, Robbe-Grillet's attitude is not at all the tragic solipsism of exquisite sensitivity which looms so large in the liberal tradition; it is slightly mitigated nihilism, derived from a technological mistrust of subjectivity, and combined with a sensitivity towards a schizoid-paranoid mode of perception. It must be evident that nothing pejorative is meant, here, by terms which, though they have a psychopathological use, also describe the irrational ways in which the mind (which only *contrives* to be rational), functions. It must also be evident that whenever one writes of an artist's work one writes of the artist's *persona*, not of the man who is also an artist. By the same token, critical activity is often a paranoid-schizoid activity, in that the critic isolates and examines, suspiciously, various aspects of the artist's creation, just as Robbe-Grillet isolates and examines, suspiciously, the content of perception. The fact that our most popular classifications of irrational thought carry pathological overtones is an indictment of our verbal culture rather than of Robbe-Grillet on one hand or the critic on the other. Indeed, it is quite arguable that the most interesting aspect of Robbe-Grillet's work is just this lyrical rendition of a mode of sensitivity akin to the alienation syndrome in Moravia, Antonioni and Godard. If Robbe-Grillet fascinates the literary world almost as much as he horrifies it, it is not only because of his poetic merits but because his denuded style paraphrases our sense of the weakness with which we are able to grasp both the world around and the life-force within. For the traditional bourgeois dismissal of all touchstones but rationalism and individualism, its reliance on the most rarefied conscious feelings of a tiny minority of well-educated and class-bound individuals, gives it a certain butterfly frailty, beautifully portrayed, in literary terms, by Virginia Woolf.

Given their common palpation of perception, one might expect Robbe-Grillet to be the heir of Virginia Woolf, with his obsessional-scientific angle related to contemporary sensibilities. But the barrier posed to her delicately intense evocation of the half-felt by his dogmatic superstructures reduces his work to the literary equivalent of Eysenckian mechanisms, and the heir to Virginia Woolf is Marguerite Duras, whose *Hiroshima Mon Amour* brings us back to Franju's 'counterpart', Alain Resnais. *Marienbad* is by Alain Resnais out of Alain Robbe-Grillet, and the latter's movie, *L'Immortelle*, reminds us that the quality of *Marienbad* derives from Resnais' extraordinary subtlety in the enrichment of his scenarios. Resnais'

21

Muriel, with its themes of memory, amnesia and illusion, and with its stylistic (i.e. perceptual) finesse, reveals affinities with Virginia Woolf; while, as we shall see, the construction of many Franju films reveals a quite conscious fascination with the temporal fragility of being.

Without in any way endeavouring to equate conscious 'sensitivity' with unconscious nihilism, it is probably true that the equivalent, on the sensitive level, of nihilism is to argue that, since reality is as various as the minds that interpret it, and since those minds are also mysteriously evasive, the appropriate attitude towards any form of commitment (political, or moral, or spiritual, or just action) is a mixture, in various proportions, of worried scepticism and unfeeling complacency—giving such forms as 'We cultured people suffer more than ordinary people because we are so much more sensitive; the lower classes should do our suffering for us.' The argument that takes us from sensitive individualism through solipsism to nihilism is by no means to be ignored, and unerringly torpedoes many of the conventional assumptions of the liberal consensus ('every man's death diminishes me', 'we are all guilty', etc.). Its main defect is probably that it is argued from an elitist sensitivity to consciousness rather than from a 'democratic' sense of conflicting libidos. In two ways, it cuts off possibilities of communication. First, its model for communication is in 'explained awareness' rather than collaborative activity or response to need. It can't conceive community activity, except as an exquisite adjustment between individual peculiarities. Thus alienation is cruelly intensified. Second, it often carries the implication that we can't expect to find, in others, enough experience roughly analogous to our own to permit spiritually satisfying degrees of recognition, of vicarious experience,

and of objective reality (even philosophical doubters agree that trains can run on time). In Resnais, an elegiac tension arises from the quiet conflict between solipsistic sadness (loneliness, forgetting) and commitment. Franju translates a similar tension into stylistic terms, whence his superimposition of the documentary, subtractive and expressionistic approaches to reality. His is almost a middle position between Robbe-Grillet and the old humanism, which Robbe-Grillet reproached for its anthropomorphic sentimentalities. Franju, calmly, notes the absence of those sentimentalities in practice. But he notes that absence sadly. This attitude is both more humanist than Robbe-Grillet's, and the only response to it. For though the universe may not be humanist, man *could* be. Hence Franju is respecting objective reality when he allows his landscapes to be sounding-boards for his characters', for his own, pain and despair.

Unexpected as it may seem, Franju's sensibility can be considered as an inversion of that underlying Robbe-Grillet's earlier novels. There, Robbe-Grillet is concerned with expurgating all emotion from his descriptions. In other words, scientific doubt is used to create a kind of schizophrenic emptiness; and, to the extent that it represents a profoundly hostile suspicion of all emotion, a suspicion of a crude and unnuanced type, it is reasonable to call it paranoid. A reader who doesn't dismiss the novels out of hand, and whose responses haven't been dimmed by the author's theories, comes to feel, underlying this style and implied by it, a sense of dread. But this dread is only implied; it is faint and unexamined; it exists without the knowledge of its author, who is a poet despite himself, and not in the least scientific.

Franju's style is also expurgatory, in ridding objects and scenes of their conventional associations. But what is substituted is not emptiness, but *new*, sharper feelings of solitude, of pain, of bleakness, of possible liberation through strangeness and poetry. It is still a very paranoid world, in its vision of humanity gripped by society and never finding liberation —just as Buñuel's characters constantly mistake a sterile rebellion for freedom and are at best still in danger. Franju's world is drenched in an atmosphere of suffering; in contrast to Robbe-Grillet the schizophrenic separation has not occurred. Inner and outer worlds, perception and emotion, are still linked. The world seems tragic, or strange, or beautiful, not because it *is*, in itself, but because it still has meaning for the human beings within it. Franju remains a pessimistic humanist, where Robbe-Grillet, offering the scientific, substitutes the nihilist. But both live in worlds of persecution and splitting: the syndrome is that described in R. D. Laing's studies in schizophrenia.

One can draw a parallel comparison between Godard and Franju. Godard's films, like Robbe-Grillet's novels, fall, though more narrowly, on the nihilist side of the divide. The fact that in their best works both artists are tragedians, underlines the assumptions which they share in opposition to the liberal-complacent consensus. Godard's treatment of tragedy depends on the real tragedy being the facility with which his characters jettison their concern with a flip shrug. His treatment of physical suffering is extremely abstract, as if to catch a blend of the abstract, the distant, and the derisory that is rhetorically effective. He deploys all sorts of interesting cinematic devices to portray the confusions of real and counterfeit experience (books, record-covers, etc); his films are in the key of white. In Franju, the possibilities of emotional pain are endless; physical suffering is exceptionally concrete; disruptions are used to explode the counterfeit; his films are in the key of black.

In a sense, Franju's and Godard's films are the lining of each other's worlds.

Merely isolating an object from its usual context rarely separates it from all its usual associations; they adhere to it in the spectator's mind and appear to be intrinsic. They can be dispersed only by new associations. This is why Franju's attitudes are extremely revolutionary whereas Robbe-Grillet's are absolutely ambiguous. Franju is more revolutionary because he is more traditional (as one avant-garde succeeds another, the paradox is becoming more and more familiar). What pop art theory sometimes describes as the isolation of an object is more usually a process of re-situating it, for example, in an art-gallery context. Equally Franju's barge in *Le Sang des Bêtes*, being abstracted from water, possesses its own movement more intensely; but also being placed in a field, it simultaneously acquires the uncanniness of drifting through solid earth.

This contradictoriness is badly needed, so tenacious are conventional associations. It takes extremely sad, cold photography to cancel out the intrinsic glamour of the Parisian monuments on which *Hôtel des Invalides* opens. Indeed, the spectator's convention-prompted attempt still to see them as romantic, probably explains why many critics mistake style for convention and see the photography as neutral, or as conventional travelogue, when in fact it's extremely depressed. The less sympathetic spectator may even appreciate Franju's stiff-upper-lip style, finding in it the restraint which affirms a *true* nobility.

Music offers another channel for resituation, and Franju's use of it is discreet and complex. Ominous music would reinforce the photographic effect, but Franju favours tunes whose wistfulness blends with a certain lilt and sparkle. It was Franju who conceived the idea of accompanying the smashed bronze bust of a war hero with a polka, and Franju who assured the composer that the lilt would enhance, rather than shatter, the mood. Often, the music's gentle glitter speaks of a sharp joy, contrasting with the solemn subjects or impersonal scenes and the sombre photography. Background music is replaced by *counterpoint* music. Indeed, music and photography often symbolize the spiritual polarity of Franju's inspiration. The photography imbues the world with sullenness, with melancholy, with a tense loneliness, a humbled sadness, with the horror of experience. The music creates a childlike freshness, a hope of joy, a nostalgia for innocence—not that it is banal: Jarre's music has its dissonances and the rhythms have an instability verging on madness. Often, Jarre's lilting tunes cannot graft on the images, they slip and slide icily from them. The music can unite with the images only through certain symbols of Franju's poetic iconography (Edith Scob, doves). This eerie combination-disjunction of joy and bitterness finds its counterpart in Franju's adumbration of a fresh alert awareness and not optimism, but an obstinate stoicism: a fully human moral stance, perhaps the most mature of which man is capable.

Photograph: Franju directing Le T.N.P.

A Cool Expressionism

Franju's cinematic preferences express his own affinities: '[I was] asked which . . . was the most intensely poetic film, and I quoted Buñuel; which was the most beautiful horror film, and I quoted Murnau; which was the most intensely graphic film, and I quoted Lang.' He feels himself close to some of the expressionist films of Germany's Golden Age, especially those of the 'Jewish school', Murnau and Lang. He once said: '*Caligari* is execrable, Murnau is *génial.* The atmosphere of realism in terror which charms him there is near his own atmosphere of realism in tragedy, and indeed his favourite cameramen, Fradetal and Schufftan, were both formed in that school. The affinities strengthen one's feelings that the atmospheric transmutation of the world by his style links with the expressionistic urge. Expressionism is still unfashionable, in our 'cool' era, unless it expresses the absurd. A word or two on expressionism may clarify its relevance to Franju.

Among film critics, expressionism is traditionally considered as the negation of realism. The term calls to mind U.F.A's huge studios, as hermetically sealed from the light of day as the dreamer's brain, with their constructed decor, archetypal or mythical plots, everything which might seem to preclude

Franju's social interests and location filming. But Murnau anticipated Franju's gift for transforming locations: much of *Nosferatu* was filmed in the streets of Hamburg, and *Tabu* consists largely of location material. In France, the expressionistic urge was closely interwoven with realism: Jean Epstein turned from expressionism to documentaries in the 'twenties, and his *La Chute de la Maison Usher* intercuts expressionistic sets and location material to interesting effect. Neither is it accidental that Mayer's script for *The Last Laugh* has all the characteristics of Zavattini's technique, but with a uniform instead of a bicycle.

In the context of literature and painting, the term expressionist may evoke the occasionally adolescent, or sentimental, stridency, with which some German artists between about 1890 and 1930 asserted cosmic metaphysical conflicts, often in consequence ignoring, oversimplifying, or caricaturing social processes and pressures out of all recognition. This expressionism can also be considered as late romanticism, which in the era of Bismarck and Krupp could no longer escape into communion with nature, or into pipe-dreams of decadence, or into realms of pure spirit, i.e. symbolism. So it was poured either into metaphysical topics —the forces of destiny, or nature, or an apocalyptic neo-Christianity—or into passionate meditations upon society. In that case, it became a romantic parallel to Marxism—sometimes a rival, sometimes an ally.

The generalised or stylised ways in which social problems were evoked may sometimes have reflected egoistic torments rather than social ones, but even then, the degree of remoteness or inaccuracy was no greater than that between our Theatre of the Absurd and the actual experiences in us to which it refers. And if the intensity with which social processes are transformed into nightmare images sometimes suggests a private malignity of inspiration, the society inspiring this dreamwork did conclude in the real nightmare of the Third Reich.

French expressionism is lightened, or diluted, by impressionist interests and a more realistic strain (from French rationalism as against German romanticism), but expressionism had its French outriders like Artaud. In the sense that expressionism is para-romanticism, Dada and Surrealism can be considered as, among other things, para-expressionist: Dada is a frenzied, gaga mimicking of conventional idiocies; Surrealism allows an outpouring of all those psychic elements which society excludes and seeks to dessicate. If, *reculant pour mieux sauter*, it rediscovers inner space it is in order to find the psychological bases for a new society, to build it on profound psychological need, a para-expressionist hope. Again the concern with society reappears. It's no accident that the Surrealists allied themselves with the Communists and split, with them and within themselves, on political issues. If, today, the Theatre of Cruelty is para-expressionist, and the Theatre of the Absurd is para-dada, Robbe-Grillet might be described as a novelist of the Absurd, despite himself.

The French poetic realism of the 'thirties has its expressionist undertow in Vigo's *L'Atalante* and *Zéro de Conduite*, in the poetic symbolism of Prévert and the moody industrial *grisailles* of Carné which merged into such masterpieces as *Le Jour se lève* and *Quai des Brumes*. Franju continues that idiom and tonality. Indeed, he is almost of that generation: he was born seven years after Vigo, three after Carné. His *Mon Chien* is scripted by Prévert; the music for *Le Sang des Bêtes* and *En Passant par la Lorraine* is by Prévert's collaborator, Kosma.

Every generation of artists manufactures, not only to its own idiom, but also its own iconography, and Franju's imagery is a survival of the 'thirties. The barges which recur in his films are like mute, captive sisters of Vigo's

L'Atalante. The pigeons circling *L'Hôtel des Invalides* or dying of cold among the gargoyles of *Notre Dame*, the doves alighting on Christiane's arms at the end of *Les Yeux sans Visage*, the crows of ill presage, and the owl which is the incarnation of the castle's soul in *Pleins Feux sur l'Assassin* recall the birds of Prévert's films and poems. In both Prévert and Franju, the child figure recurs, an incarnation of non-puritanical, amoral innocence.

Chronologically, though, Franju's nearer contemporaries are Clouzot and Clément, who established themselves in features in the early 'forties, and the black realism of his films is evocative of theirs—though tragic, rather than cynical. But his heavily oppressive style, his emphasis on pain, recall another realistic director who is also heavily indebted to expressionism. Andrzej Wajda's *Kanal* and *Ashes and Diamonds* share with Franju's films a fatalistic air, a slow rhythm, a sense of heroes lost in labyrinthine traps, and a visual quality con-

Photograph: director as magician—Franju and the dove which is brought back to life by the hawk in Judex.

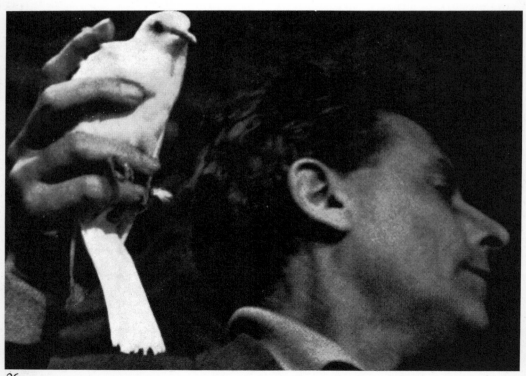

stantly evoking the phrase coined to describe Swift by Aldous Huxley: 'the excremental vision'.

If German expressionism was hysterical, Franju's is obsessional. The seeds of Teutonic sentimentality about purity, innocence and redemption, versus the demonic and the corrupt, are clear enough in the Franju fetishes of innocence, but only one of his films (*Mon Chien*) is overly sentimental and that in a far less radical way. The forces of purity never take a Messianic role; the contrasts never become Manichean, for the action involves on everyone's part all the impure and mediocre vices and virtues. Nor, of course, has purity here anything to do with its Christian moral senses, of virginity, altruism, disinterestedness, etc. It refers, rather, to potentialities of tenderness, of which Edith Scob is so often the incarnation. With her alert, gentle eyes, her child's forehead, the lightly maternal gestures of her hands, she is the personification of the lilting music. She resembles at once a child, a bird, a mother; her tenderness is in itself both erotic and angelic. Indeed, to speak of her as a symbol is to suggest something far more schematic than the delicacy that makes her as subtle and haunting a figure as Giulietta Masina or Louise Brooks, a Kwan-Yin to Barbara Steele's Kali. To be sure, the key of erotic tenderness is atypical of the modern cinema, and finds almost its last screen celebration in Borzage's *Moonrise;* again, Franju's films reveal their archaism, their nostalgia. 'As Cocteau says of Thomas—I'm quoting from memory—"He could neither swim nor skate. But he could say: I'm swimming, or I'm skating. And everyone had seen him on the ice and in the waves." Edith Scob has the same gift. . . . She is very precious. She is a magic person. She gives the unreal reality.' But if, for Franju, this erotic tenderness is the light of the world, the affirmation includes no mystification, no escapism, no metaphysic, no optimism.

The Surrealism of Science

Franju's realism extends to his conception of the medium. 'Any screen image has an immediate presence. Whatever you do, a film is always in the present tense. The past is spontaneously reactualised by the spectator. That's why anything artificial ages quickly and badly. Dreams, poetry, the fantastic must emerge from reality itself. Every film is a documentary, even the most poetic.' After all, the most outrageous fantasy is simply a documentary of somebody's outrageous fantasies, and needs to catch their *real*, subjective, life. Conversely, poetry, far from arising in some super-civilized portion of our brain, is as matter-of-fact as lava flowing from the crater of an active volcano. Indeed, one must be on one's guard against that reverence for poetry which is poetry's deadliest, because most insidious, enemy (just as putting a flower in a vase to admire it is also to murder it; poetry, like roses, prefers earth, and manure, to cut glass). Perhaps that's why Keats, remarking that poetry must come as naturally as the leaves on the tree, added darkly, 'or it had better not come at all.' The deadliest enemy of poetry is 'poeticism'. Just as Richard Strauss has incessantly to put his singers on their guard against 'beautifying the beautiful, gilding the lily', so Franju reiterates: 'You can't set out to make films with the intention of being poetic. Or if I say I'm going to make a philosophical film, I'm just being ridiculous. What I'll make is a film from which philosophical conclusions can be drawn.' Since poetry and philosophy both have their roots in one's conception of reality, simply to render that conception of reality is the true path to true poetry. 'Feuillade's realism is all the more beautiful because he wasn't trying to be aesthetic. . . . Buñuel used to say that the "magical" could exist in bad films just as keenly as in good films, and that links . . . with the lecture André Breton and I wanted to give on those fragments of bad films which correspond to surrealist notions, so that despite the intentions of directors, cinematographic poetry tends to rise up and come to the surface.'

When the will to poetry is academic rather than organic, the result is as grotesque as if you try to 'get that quality of the fantastic by concocting some Frankenstein Monster and plonking electrodes on his head . . . [poetry] . . . is simpler and subtler.' To Breton's 'Beauty is convulsive or it will not be', Franju might have added: 'Poetry is compulsive and involuntary or it will not be.' As he says of a shot of a line of poplars riding a crest and lit by the lights of passing cars in *La Tête contre les Murs:* 'it's ghostlike and it's extraordinary because it's always there, yet you don't see it as you pass by.' Such insights require more than mere sensibility; if there is poetry in brutality, it is simply because the poetry is the act of really seeing. The pang of beauty is not an idiot adoration of what's seen but the shock of tearing the veil, of ripping off one's own spiritual skin. The only poetry which matters is that which cuts to the quick. Franju comes very near Bataille's view that beauty's mainspring is the breaking of tabu, when he reminisces over an old friend who was clearly a man after his own heart:

'The other day I met my old projectionist from the Musée de l'Homme. "M. Franju!", he said, "we haven't seen each other for nineteen years. Do you remember that surgical film which had twenty people flat out on the floor?" Nineteen years later, he still remembered that one! And he'd got used to gruelling films there. The film was Dr Thierry de Martel's *Trépanation pour crise d'épilepsie Bravais-Jacksonnienne.* That was an authentic horror film, twenty people were out flat, I've never seen anything so drastic. It was an atrocious film, but a beautiful and poetic one, because it was also realistic.' Indeed, Franju's own analysis of the film throws a good deal of light on his own style:

'. . . plastic values, the macabre, and poetry, have never been sparked off in unison together with all the efficacy of realism and the beauty of Surrealism, as, by pure chance, in a film in which no-one even wanted them. . . .

'The division of this realistic drama in colour into operating periods—like acts—, its progression, its strange *mise-en-scène*—the patient, instead of lying down, is sitting up—and above all his behaviour (his "acting") are all the more frightening for the spectator in that he hasn't even the reassurance of clearly seeing the victim's face. So his suffering and the fear of the spectator are undivided. He's hardly to know that, after he has all but fainted away, and is rising from his seat to leave the cinema, the surgeon-commentator will appear on the screen to inform him that the skull, which he saw being worked on with trepanning tools, with probes, scalpels and saws, was insensitised to pain. And the patient, with his pallid countenance reddened by the iodine that has poured down from his skull . . . looks right into the camera, at the suffering spectator, and smiles. And since that operation has a happy end, can't we say that that constitutes a memorable gag; a brilliant touch of black comedy?'

And, after all, what more Surrealist than

those scientific films which translate into visually perceptible forms the sectors, levels or patterns of reality which, with authority, undermine the framework constructed by our socially-conditioned perceptions, usually miscalled 'realism'? This, rather than subtractionism or the laborious purgation of the anthropomorphism in perception, is the real and the most effective response to scientific culture, which in itself is not a threat to the imagination, but as powerful a catalyst as STP. And Franju's long association with scientific films may have fostered that ability to stay and watch, quietly, throughout those terrible moments of violence which 'don't bear thinking about'. It is the compassion of the good doctor or nurse, who must neither avert his eyes nor cease caring.

Still: business efficiency at work in Le Sang des Bêtes.

Love that Brute

If Franju's attitude is a synthesis of the compassionate and the steely, he unabashedly admits to 'a certain taste for violence which enabled me to express myself in *Le Sang des Bêtes*.' The slaughterhouses are there, of course, for those whose taste is merely for the fruits of violence, and whose innocence is thoroughly artificial, i.e. callous, because it results from carefully repressing any natural curiosity as to just how that chop quit the pig for the plate (no doubt it just ripened and fell off, like a peach?). If our natural curiosity hadn't been carefully repressed, we should quite naturally be very interested in what happens in slaughterhouses, and go and have a look, and not need films like *Le Sang des Bêtes*: nor, indeed, art, which is, after all, the spiritual equivalent of National Health spectacles.

Whether Franju's taste for violence is the consequence of a genuinely innocent curiosity, as his connection with scientific films might suggest, whether it arises from a fascination, which, far from being morbid, is the natural result of fundamental and not merely conventional human tabus, whether it is Sadistic (in the philosophical sense), or even sadistic (in the vulgar sense) is neither here nor there. As the police-chief says to Buñuel's Archibaldo de la Cruz, 'If we arrested everybody who'd ever committed a crime in his imagination, there'd be more people in prison than out.' The real distinction is between those whose reason for not committing the crime is fear of being found out, whether by the police, their neighbours, or their God, and those whose reason for refraining is an *aristocratic* reason: pride in themselves, or respect or sympathy for others.

Is it even conceivable that a little more conscious sadism would diminish the terrible voracity of today's impersonal killing techniques —H-bombs, napalm—a voracity which almost seems to fit Freud's formulation that the higher the degree of repression the more insatiable is the obsession for ever less satisfying forms of gratification? After all, civilized sexuality seems to be following the same course. . . . Possibly not; possibly man's perennial violence springs as much from his ability to reason as from his lack of it. Unlike an animal he can constantly see the limits of his power; unlike an animal he is perpetually frightened, although too, like an animal, he can't reason clearly enough to fear only the real dangers.

Even so, a degree of conscious sadism sufficient to relish elaborate imaginings (like those of Archibaldo de la Cruz—or of most filmgoers!) may be far less dangerous than an excess of unconscious sadism, the defences against which lead to self-righteousness, as the sadism is denied in oneself, and exaggerated fear or paranoia, as the sadism is attributed to others. This very process leads to a common abuse of Freudian theory, whereby it is supposed that anyone who has, say, two sadistic thoughts a day, must have more unconscious sadism breaking through than someone who has only one sadistic thought a day. The assumption here is that all sadism must be breaking through from the unconscious or the irrational (though if sadism is the will to power, much of it is neither unconscious nor irrational). This assumption explains why Pamela Hansford Johnson's attempt to blame the Moors murder case on the lack of literary censorship finds such an echo in liberal fainthearts. But, from our viewpoint, it wasn't the books that fostered the sadism, but the sadism that chose the books, and there are many other reasons for choosing the same books, including the conscious coming to terms with one's own sadism.

Obviously, no-one has no sadism in his unconsciousness; it's a matter of the relative strength of sadism and love, for the two often go together; a great love may arouse peculiar mixtures of sadism and tenderness. Indeed, to feel no twinge of identification with power would be schizophrenic, an only incidentally altruistic form of psychopathology. From this point of view, a conscious sadism, a certain taste for violence, may be no more than an inoculation against squeamishness. The films themselves confirm Franju's reiterated claim that his interest is in the victim, that he is on the side of the victim, whether it's a white horse in a slaughterhouse, a salmon with the hook tearing at its mouth, a war cripple with shrapnel-twisted lips, or a mental patient staring at the wall. On *La Tête contre les Murs*, he remarked, 'When I have to deal with a sick person, I become tender and not at all sadistic, not that there's the least difference anyway', and this reading of Sade concurs with our formulation that the man whose sadism is in his conscious mind will be less frightened of others than the man whose sadism is unconscious or who's idiot enough to think he's devoid of sadism. It also evokes the figure of Sade in Peter Weiss's play: when the frightened guards threaten a dangerous lunatic with their bludgeons, Sade can calm him, tenderly.

At any rate, in a period when critics are hypochondriac about mass media violence, Franju's most violent films, with one exception, have never been accused of relishing violence,

or, indeed, of being conducive to anything but a convulsive intensification of saturnine compassion. If Franju's art is much possessed by *thanatos*, by suffering, madness, violence and dying, it is because *thanatos* is the new obscenity, and, like all obscenities, inalienable to man.

It is easy enough to be tender in erotic or amiable circumstances, and so pessimism frightens us. We associate it with a carapace of indifference, of inhumanity; we assume that if we really saw violence, it would make us brutal, rather than tender, that if we really thought about death, it would make us give up, rather than cherish others and ourselves. Hence the desperate rarity and the almost prophetic power of artists who, like Franju, can remain tender in the face of brutality and loss, who can maintain a tender pessimism. As Franju has commented, his most violent films are the most tender, because the more tender you are the more you feel the violence, and it's in the face of violence that tenderness is most extreme. Franju's is not at all a savage eye; his toughness is stoic, his vision as tender as can bear the truth.

Still: Les Yeux sans Visage.

The Films

Le Métro, Le Sang des Bêtes

Le Métro

Franju's first film, co-directed with Henri Langlois, precedes his second by fifteen years, and seems to have been something of a false start. It was financed by Langlois's family, and made on 16 millimetre, a genre technically more indigent than now, with a borrowed, fixed-focus camera. The fullest critical account of it is Henri Agel's: 'Clearly Franju, in 1934, the date of Le Métro, had yet to achieve either mastery or originality of expression. This essay, which is a rather sympathetic one, evokes at once Entr'acte and the whole avant-garde of the 1925 era. The abruptness of the editing, the hunt for angles, are elements of a rhetoric which the artist was to renounce almost entirely. But let us recall in particular the taste for certain very long-held shots (legs descending stairs) which heralds the deliberately slow pace of his subsequent films.'

Le Sang des Bêtes

In a wasteland, old goods are heaped for sale. Grey rubble and grey sky stretch away beyond a dining-room table in solid oak, and an electric lamp hangs from the branches of a tree. Each item remembers, recreates, the room around it. Furnishing and setting between them create a double image of house and horizon, akin to certain paintings of Magritte.

A building rears up before the camera, its bleak brick asserting all the utilitarian impersonality of the nineteenth century. It might be a prison, a warehouse, a cotton mill, a pickle factory.

Among the tools of its trade are the poleaxe, the spike, the humane killer, tools which its craftsmen wield with skill and pride.

A meek white carthorse rears back under the impact of a humane killer, stumbles, kneels, keels over. A spike is plunged deep into its neck, and a torrent of blood gushes steaming

32

forth. Round the prone bulk men bustle and hack, and in a few moments the carcass is dismembered.

To paralyse their reflexes (for threshing and flailing spoils meat), and secondarily to anaesthetise them, cows have long steel spikes banged through their skulls into their brains.

Calves with their throats cut judder about so obstinately that their kicking heads send the pans of their hot blood skidding and slopping across the tiled floor; men have to restrain their posthumous vivacity.

A butcher saws through a cow's hanging carcass in the time it takes for the town hall clock to strike mid-day.

Knee-deep in blood, the craftsmen sing popular songs, among them the Charles Trenet hit, *La Mer*.

Sheep are dismembered, their heads and feet put on separate stacks. Row upon row of legs kick furiously.

The film ends by returning us to a city whose grey, inarticulate stone is infused with the sadness of all industrial concentrations.

The film's form is not simply that of prologue, 'body' and coda, but also that of thesis (the sad city), a terrible antithesis (the slaughterhouse), and the synthesis (the coalescence, in our minds, of the two).

This schema fairly summarises the film's structure, but if the last statement closes in on us with teeth like a mantrap's it's because, during the central section, Franju has found formal or poetic pretexts to cut away from the slaughterhouse to the city which it feeds. It's not simply that Franju has a delicate ear for contrasts, nor simply that, with macabre showmanship, he avoids piling shock upon shock, without relief, in case he eventually stunned, or even inured, us. These formulations suggest that every shot that's not violent is merely a breathing-space between those that are. But the 'intermediate' shots have two positive func-

tions. If Franju intersperses the paroxysmic sequences with asides of an elegiac and/or ironic nature it is to resensitize the spectator, and therefore his response to violence; it is with his finer fibres that he bears the shock. The cutaways repoeticize, they reintellectualize, and they reassert that the slaughterhouse and the city are an entity, like spider and spider's web. As the virtuoso butcher hacks at the cow's hung carcass, and the clock strikes twelve, shots of various aspects of the city synchronize with the strokes. After the final disposal of the white horse, we return to the outside world to see a flock of white sheep being led across a canal: 'their bleating is like the singing of hostages' (if the comparison seems slightly forced, it is no doubt less so to those who have heard hostages' songs in just such streets). Two nuns walk up to the slaughterhouse gates, their headdresses like seagulls, knock on the door and beg for offal. At first sight, the film's climactic violence is its positive pole, the quieter shots the negative. But, from another angle, it is the quieter shots which constitute the film's, and the spectator's, home key.

Franju cheerfully explains the secret of his film's opening. 'In fiction, fantasy is usually obtained by giving the artificial (studio decor, etc.) the appearance of reality. In our films we set out to restore to documentary realism its actual quality of apparently artificial decor. We managed it by shooting buildings from directly in front (like the Moulin de Panton) or else we chose houses with sharp profiles (at the Port du Flandre) and avoided any hint of depth ... Whether in the business of the barge emerging "in" the wasteland ... like a theatre flat, or with those trees which look like theatre props, we were constantly preoccupied with expressing the plastic character of the decor, and we often waited for several days for the weather to be simultaneously diffuse (misty) and dense in the sky, or else for everything to

33

be lit up with that particular, local colour which strikes one as a freak of the sunlight. . . .'

The violent scenes are no less sensitively observed (although the subject matter is likely to pre-empt the spectator's conscious attention). 'The choice of the month of November for shooting the interiors was dictated by the fact that at this season of the year the animals are slaughtered by electric light, and the blood steaming in the glacial cold of the scalding bays allowed us, despite all the technical problems, to compose our images. . . .'

This unvarying sensitivity, not simply to aesthetics, but to reality, enables a double image, analogous to that of the home-wasteland, to reappear in the heart of the violence: in Henri Agel's words, 'the ordering of the dismemberments takes on an almost ritual character, the stunned horse falls in a curtsey, while the killers, bathed in vapours of blood, seem to officiate. . . .'

'It's for the sake of aesthetic realism that I chose a childlike girl's voice, confidential and lightly overcast like the weather, to speak over the exteriors the rigorous, moving and sometimes ironic commentary of Jean Painlevé.' It's not altogether a coincidence that Nicole Ladmiral, who speaks the commentary, also plays Chantal in Bresson's *Journal d'un Curé de Campagne*, for a common personality often implies a common mood; and the effect of the grey, unemphatic voice is akin to Bresson's when he requires his actors to speak their lines without responding to the meaning in them. But for neither Franju nor for Bresson's case is this actually expressionless—the voice has its key, its mood; the fact of a girl's voice is itself a statement, its tone of quietly sad, passive matter-of-factness is another: anything more would 'beautify the beautiful', and lose the mesmerism of the factualness.

Similarly, in the heart of the atrocious, one doesn't merely note, one is profoundly affected by the deftness and speed of the butchers; we *see* it so clearly that, for all the crosscurrents in us of (misdirected) anger and tragic irony, we can share their legitimate pride in their skill, do justice to the moral neutrality of their song, to their own qualities as victims. The butchers never become scapegoats, and so refract our disquiet back from them to the system of which the audience is also a part.

Most spectators remember the film as an intense experience, but usually, it seems, in a very abstract way. They have a lively memory of its overall effect, but ask them to describe specific scenes, and they can remember only one or two—usually the white horse, presumably because it possesses overtones of iconographic sentimentality, and because it is the film's first shock. Very few people remember from films, or novels for that matter, more than a mood and a few 'snapshots', but it's surprising that the same amnesia should operate in the case of a film so vivid that it brings some people near the point of fainting. One would expect the 'horror' images to be branded upon the mind. Perhaps this forgetting is a sort of fainting. Perhaps, too, the fact that the film is remembered emotionally rather than visually suggests that its effect is as much a matter of structure and counterpoint as of raw visual realism *per se*. Sometimes, too, people remember the peripheral shots, where the horror imbues and is dilated by the everyday, where the Paris skies rumble with ominous gradations of grey, and its sullen mass flickers with the sadly starting flocks of birds.

The constant interpenetration of finesse and violence so attunes our imagination as to impregnate with special meanings scenes on which no comment need even be implied. The shot of the sheep crossing the bridge into the

Still: Le Sang des Bêtes—*the death of* Crin Blanc.

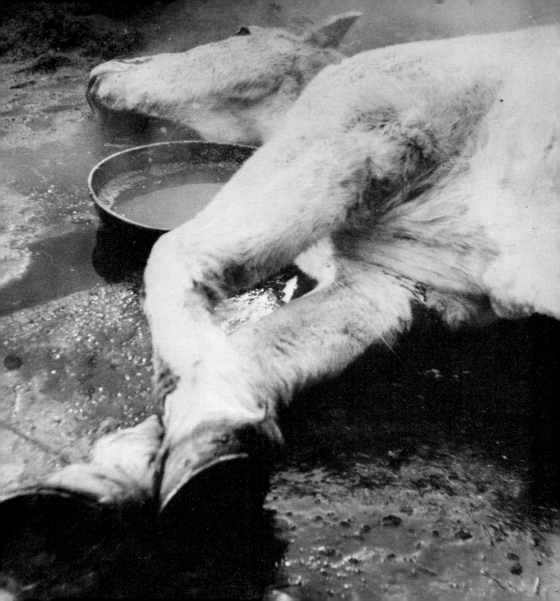

slaughterhouse, scenting blood, reluctant to enter, but reassured by 'leaders' specially planted by their shepherds, can't but recall the words of the 23rd Psalm. The Lord may be one's shepherd, he may feed one and make one down to lie in green pastures, but he may also lead one into clean slaughterhouses. Blake objected to shepherds who shear the faithful of their fleece, but even stronger objections are appropriate for a God whose intentions are to reduce one to the spiritual equivalent of meat. In any case, do shepherds really love their flock (except collectively), would they lay down their life for it (except inadvertently)? Similarly, Agel seems to have missed the point about the sacrificial overtones to the slaughter. Given Franju's anticlericalism, it's hardly likely to be, as Agel's description suggests it can be taken as being, that butchers are in a sense the priests of life's eternal tragedy, that the animals are, in a kind of pantheistic communion, sacrifically allowing their life-force to be transubstantiated into man, who, as a spiritually higher creature, is capable of grasping God on behalf of the lower animals too. On the contrary: Franju's parable is a warning of the folly of all blind, habitual obedience to those set in authority over us, for our own good, of course. The overtones don't transform the executioners into priests; the metaphor flows the other way; next time you see a priest officiating at the altar, think of him as a butcher. The vibrations of the scene strike not only at Christianity, but at any number of religions or, indeed, at man's religious impulse, centred as it is on those ceremonies of sacrifice which seek to deny death, to mystify injustice into self-sacrifice, to repudiate responsibility (scapegoat symbolisms), to attain an immortal life which is only an immunity from life (i.e. the protection of death), to enjoy a mystic 'community' which doesn't exist, whereas the seas of blood through which the singing butchers stride certainly do exist.

The hacking of the carcass while the clock strikes provoked two critics to cite John Donne. For Alan Lovell, 'the set of cutaways to "our" city is an exact filmic equivalent of John Donne's "No man is an island".' And for this writer, ' "For whom the bell tolls" is given a chilling insouciance. The bell creates a dramatic solemnity, akin to a crucifixion (the hanging carcass). But instead of darkness at noon it's business as usual, or a quiet siesta while one's digestive juices soak up that steak.' The episode is a classic example of montage in the Eisensteinian sense: not because of its quick cutting, which is montage only in the debased Hollywood sense, but because the thesis (the carcass) and the antithesis (the city) produce a synthesis which is as abstruse as the phrases of a metaphysical poet. Even this dialectic yields too simple an account: for beside hung carcass/crucifixion come other 'pairs': axe-strokes/clock's strokes and so on. The meaning lies not in one dialectic, but in several, which don't so much add up to an eventual synthesis, but horizontally transform the values of individual terms. Indeed this revision of dialectics might usefully be transferred from poetic to political theory. And, to return to Eisenstein, montage consists, not in the juxtaposition of objects to produce one single meaning, but in the juxtaposition also of all their associations, including those imported by stylistic nuance, producing a bunch of meanings.

Franju is not so ascetic as to resist an extrinsic comment when it doesn't disturb his effect. Thus it is only those connoisseurs of movie technique who, in seeing a film, carefully study the synchronization of sight and sound, who will notice that the commentary is talking about nuns while an image shows the excrements of a cow. Franju's humour has its peasant flavour. But only those comments are made which, while appealing to his *amis inconnus*, often assert a blasphemous implacability against

36

that sentimental and undeserved respect for the feelings of the religious which so often reduces criticism of Christianity to something like a confession of respectful admiration. But he allows himself only those comments which, as self-effacing as certain cryptograms in music, assert no false emphasis against the film's principle impetus, which is directed at the slow dilatation of appearances until, as tender, as clumsy and as surreal as a newborn calf, reality appears. . . .

The perils of the opposite course, of a conspicuous and insistent commitment, are exemplified by a Czechoslovak picture called, in Britain, *Isn't Life Wonderful?*, or variations on that title. Its attack on the complacencies of bourgeois optimism is carried out by every effect of ironic contrast: 'Blue Skies' sung by Bing Crosby, '*C'est si bon*' by Louis Armstrong, overlaid on shots of concentration camps, the starving poor, and so on. In structure, the effect is exactly that of Franju's use of *La Mer* over a sea of blood. But there are two important differences. The butcher's song naturally arises from, exists in the situation itself; it isn't *dragged in*. Czechoslovakian contrasts, taken from here, there and everywhere, immediately take on a philosophical-political sphere of reference; being knockdown polemic, they mobilise all our polemical defences. Furthermore, the rhetorical means being almost more obvious than the ends, one is likely to resent the hectoring tone even if one agrees with it. With a whoop of triumph, all one's sales resistance seizes on its imprecision. One may agree with the attack on pop music, or on the commercial media, or American culture in general, and Western culture in general. No doubt it is extremely wicked of us to allow ourselves even one second's relaxation while suffering is going on anywhere in the world, and we ought to let our standard of living drop like a stone while we buckle to the task of helping Oxfam's teeming millions. But my immediate reaction is to reflect that the film might have been less facile and more disturbing if its expressions of our complacency had also featured high culture: Toscanini, in fine style, conducting cannons and napalm-bursts, Fonteyn-Nureyev tripping the light fantastic in *Swan Lake* while refugees tramp along dusty endless roads, the fine eloquence of Olivier compared with the cost of silence that is the real face of suffering, and so on. But however you shift the terms the contrasts are facile and static, because they're *mere* contrast. Much closer connections are needed before all the associations of each element can be brought into contact and so create the myriad subtle contrasts which result in poetry.

For all that, *Le Sang des Bêtes* can hardly be summed up, as it is constantly summed up, as a poetic vision of a slaughterhouse. For 'poetic vision' implies that there are un-poetic, common-sensical, matter-of-fact views of slaughterhouses. And it carries the further implication: 'of course, Franju is a very sensitive person, a poet—naturally, he *would* feel things acutely; but all that sensitivity is poetic and visionary, you know; it's all a matter of cultural ornaments, not of real life.' The corollary of this approach to life is the sort of poem one might find in certain literary journals—something written by a poet-tourist who, visiting a slaughterhouse, immediately thought 'I really mustn't lose this opportunity of writing a poem; after all, a slaughterhouse is a very poetic place', and stands around noting sensitive metaphors in his little book. What comes out is a densely textured little poem which richly deserves its high mark: say 99½ out of 100. But a mark is all it deserves. One recalls Stephen Spender, gazing at unemployed men begging in railway halls and vowing, 'No, I shall weave no tracery of pen-ornament/To make them birds upon my singing tree', to which the appropriate answer is, no doubt, to touch one's cloth cap and mutter, 'Cor, ta, guv'nor, yer a real toff.' The very metaphor is as neat a bit of euphuistic tracery as anything since Lyly. One could write a thesis on the peculiar passivity implied in that Spender-Auden era mannerism: 'Let . . .' (in this case 'the wrong cry out as raw as wounds'), as if the world was somehow run by a moral destiny equivalent to their old headmaster, whom they, like radical fifth formers, were petitioning. Most depressing of all is the relentless dissolution of everybody and everything into a *pointillisme* of metaphors, similes, and abstract emotive words: the result of the sensitive style is to render the unemployed thoroughly abstract and substitute for them an intricate tracery of abstractions which has the minor qualities of a political Georgianism, including moral pathos, but makes a solid, *prosaic* contact impossible.

If one imagines a slaughterhouse poem along similar lines, it's easy to imagine how our poet-tourist, more concerned, really, with his poetry than with his raw material—a symptomatic phrase—multiplies the mental and verbal suggestions, but loses the real massiveness of the main business of slaughterhouses, which is slaughter. This isn't to say that the onlooker's reality isn't *a* reality, obviously it is, nor is it to say that one can't proceed, as Franju has, from observation to empathy and insight. But it's a much less interesting reality, indeed, it can be a 'confusionist' reality, than the reality which includes both the objective and the subjective realities of slaughter. The attempt to subsume both aspects of the subject will inevitably involve one in deploying all the resources of poetic sensitivity.

Conversely, the best poetry about reality has all the prosaic virtues, works *with* the prosaic, and a step towards a new classical language is being taken with the evolution of a new poetic prose *à la* Trocchi, Kerouac, etc. For the butchers, the slaughtering is all in the day's work, so the Hamlets of this particular Prince of Denmark are the animals, for whom it's all a matter of life and death, or rather, of death. It's true that they don't know what hit them, and that the fact that 'life must go on' makes the dead uninteresting. We can all feel in ourselves the seeds of that rather terrifying viewpoint whereby the dying or the old hardly matter, whereby their feelings lie as lightly on the scale as their future, a valuation to which the old themselves often subscribe. Hence the importance of works of art which insist that even 'dead-end' experiences, even the muddled panic in a pig's brain as his misgivings intensify and suddenly his throat gets more or less deftly sliced, matter from an objective point of view. Hence the importance of not allowing pure poetry to settle for that sensitive impressionism which, while dealing admirably with all sorts of peripheral nuances and reflections, can no more catch the central shocks of the experience than you can catch a charging rhinoceros in a shrimping-net.

To some extent, the trap is easier to fall into in literature than in the cinema, since literature has to reconstruct reality from a network of abstract equivalents, words, whereas the cinema can home in more directly on the concrete and the physical. But the achievements of literature, and the pitfalls of cinema, can be symbolized by the intensely poetic prose of Hardy, or any bad film, i.e. nine films out of ten. And there is no reason in the media themselves why literature should not match or even surpass, for example, Franju's quiet presentation of the tools and tricks of the butcher's trade. Indeed, the poetry of practicality which is so often so dreadfully lacking from the spectrum of current poetry is inherent in certain technical manuals for nurses, undertakers, butchers and others whose occupations carry tabus because of their disturbing, that is, poetic reality. For example, the chapters on slaughterhouse techniques in

38

Frank Gerrard's *Meat Technology* (Leonard Hill, London, 1964) present a somewhat idealized picture, in that the account of how to do it well hardly suggests the wild messes that occur when it's not well done, and in that it's emotionally aseptic. But, poetically read, the asepticism is itself an irony, and the techniques give some insight into the anatomical infrastructure of the subjectively unspeakable, as well as carrying a respect for the practical process which gets lost in a culture whose frame of reference too rarely leaves that of the white-collar worker.

We may already have seen decapitated chickens running around as if looking everywhere for their heads, but here, locked as we are in a cinema, with only a succession of death-images to contemplate, death ceases to be a definite boundary, for the nervous system clearly has its doubts. We are gripped by the screen's tight image into an intensive identification with the dying, an identification probably more intense than we would feel if we were walking round an actual slaughterhoues, where we would need to keep a mask on our faces and could easily look away from, or not even notice, those details to which Franju relentlessly drags our attention. Now we cannot but doubt the hangman's usual apologia, to the effect that hanging (or gassing, or electrocuting) is all but painless, if not actually enjoyable. What's sauce for the goose is sauce for the human animal too, and the posthumous agitations eerily caricature, and reverse, the usual argument about souls. Maybe the space within our minds is infinitely larger than the space within our skulls, but our minds' desires and actions are firmly rooted in the biological mind-body warp constituted by our carcasses, by the lumps of meat which swell proudly beneath our shirts and strut around in our trousers. These butchers' knives cut theology's throat, and leave it bleeding to death at the back of our minds.

Given Franju's connections with the scientific film, it's fitting that the commentary for the first of his 'grand series' of documentaries should be written by Jean Painlevé, whose documentaries on vampire bats, sea-horses and sea-urchins and other bizarre modalities of the life-force plunge us into consciousnesses stranger than our wildest dreams. To see these films is to dream ourselves into biological warps which reveal our world as a reticulation of other worlds as eerie as anything in Philip José Farmer's 'The Lovers', Theodore Sturgeon's 'Venus Plus X' or Nicolas Devil's '*Les Aventures de Saga*'. What seems in retrospect even eerier is that we could ever have thought this world was familiar. No doubt your pet dog or your pet snake really loves you, in the fully human sense of the word, but what, concretely, goes on in his mind? What is the image of your dog's recognition of you?

Painlevé's science-fact can be contrasted to science-fiction, just as the natural sciences can be contrasted with metaphysics. Milton has been called an ancestor of science-fiction, in so far as he allows himself to speculate upon the digestive processes of angels. But he had never seen an angel and was working it all out from those rules which appeared to operate in the world he knew. Rationalism = extrapolation = metaphysics. The natural sciences reverse the approach. Extrapolation may yield a hypothesis, but a hypothesis is all it is until you have caught your angel and put, if not salt on its tail, at least radioactive tracers in its food, and also conducted a post-mortem. Materialism = empiricism = hypotheses. Science-fiction is the metaphysics of an age which doesn't believe in metaphysics, just as poetry is spilled religion. Indeed, science-fiction is a contemporary form of poetic myth, and its relation to science-fact (which inventions Wells predicted, etc.) is the least important thing about it. Of course science-fact and science-fiction can impregnate

39

each other, just as poetic myth is most impressive when it's 'married' to a believed cosmogony. And this is why it isn't as perverse as it may seem to indicate the progression Franju-Painlevé-Farmer, that is, the progression from Franju's *poésie matérialiste* (a phrase of Maurice Nadeau's about Prévert first applied to Franju by Freddy Buache) to *poésie scientifique* and then *poésie science-fiction*. *Le Sang des Bêtes* is to *poésie science-fiction* as *Hiroshima Mon Amour* is to *L'Année Dernière à Marienbad*. The first pair concern other modalities of consciousness as the latter pair concern the human mind's grip on memory and reality.

Painlevé's *Les Assassins de l'Eau Douce*, which shows myriad forms of freshwater life devouring one another assiduously, to the soundtrack of 'thirties swing-music, reveals that your humble pond is, among other things, a gaily relentless Auschwitz, that assassinating to absorb is also an essential link of being, a form of community; *Le Sang des Bêtes* is a parallel statement, though here the picture includes man pitching in with a will. It's curious how quickly our minds rush to console ourselves with the thought that, after all, slaughterhouses are somehow exceptional places. Maybe, but meat isn't an exceptional diet. The radical antithesis of metaphysics and materialism appears in another form. Roman Catholic theologians and their spiritual fellow-travellers are apt to reassure themselves with the dogma that since animals have no souls, God isn't perplexed by the fact that men kill them to eat, whereas he would be perplexed if men had to eat men to live. Indeed if cannibalism is mythically so interesting, it's because the slide from animal to human meat is so easy that early and massive tabus are needed to block it, and the rites of the last supper derive their poig-

Still: Le Sang des Bêtes. *The grey veils of everyday routines.*

40

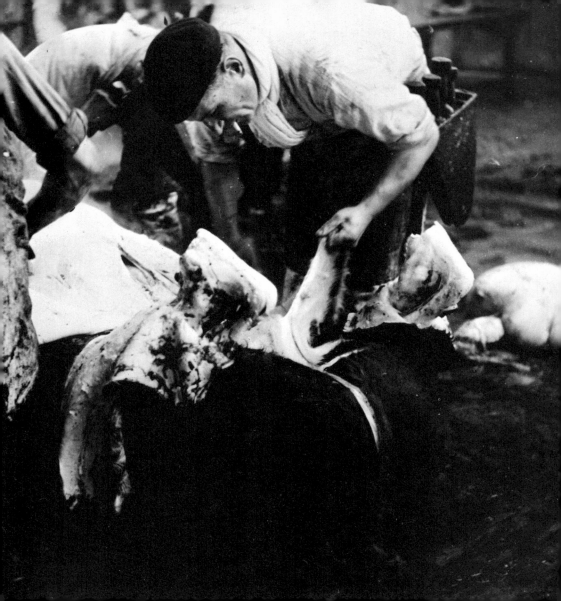

nancy from evoking just that impulse, faintly, and in an ethically beautiful form. Ironically, therefore, it's not the Roman Catholic church, but Brigitte Bardot, who cares about man's unnecessary inhumanity to animals in slaughterhouses. It's enough to make the mythical St Francis of Assisi turn in his grave, though the historical St Francis was pretty callous himself.

Not that Franju's holy rage at the carnivorous aspects of existence is meant to make us vegetarians, still less to paralyse us with guilt. Rather, it's a reminder that what is inevitable may also be spiritually unendurable, that what is justifiable may be atrocious, that the best we can do will always be an organized butchery—and the possible best is itself light-years from fulfilment. Only when we have realised that, like our Mad Mother Nature, our Mad Father Society is an organization of deaths as well as of lives, can we become more aware, gentle, alive, sad, free for a Schweitzerian reverence for life, i.e. a reverence for all lives, and not just the next one. The road to spiritual maturity leads, not upwards into the clouds, but downwards, into a relentless materialism.

Whether to develop or refute it, scarcely a critic has ever resisted the comparison between Franju's *Le Sang des Bêtes* and Resnais' *Nuit et Brouillard*, that is, between the slaughterhouses for animals and the slaughterhouses for men. The town-hall clock strikes twelve as a craftsman hacks, that hacking becomes the city centre; the church spires nestle prettily in the green countryside round Buchenwald. A butcher sings *La Mer*, camp orchestras strike up marches from musical comedy. Above all, the tone is reminiscent: the tenderness, the finesse, the avoidance of easy indignation.

Still: The mysteries of a skilled craft. Animals are turned into meat in Le Sang des Bêtes.

En Passant par la Lorraine

Franju's slaughter triptych, *Le Sang des Bêtes*, *En Passant par la Lorraine* and *Hôtel des Invalides* were all produced by a film company calling itself Forces et Voix de France. Although there does tend to be a connection between the establishment and sponsorship, the ringing patriotism of the name may well express an intention to help restore a national pride which had been badly shattered in 1940; ten years later, the younger generation was notoriously saturnine about the achievements of its elders and betters.

Franju was probably not the ideal man to change their minds for them, even though his brief must closely have paralleled those of directors who hymned the Empire Marketing Board or the various activities of the Crown. Generalisations are dangerous, and an example is only a generalisation in insidiously modest guise. Nonetheless, when all sorts of concessions and exceptions have modified the rule, there remains a certain truth in this contrast, between two documentary treatments of industrialisation. The first is one of those classic English documentaries, *Industrial Britain*, directed by Robert Flaherty in 1931; the second is *En Passant par la Lorraine*.

Flaherty's romantic tone poem about the beauty of smokescapes and factory work is keyed by the commentator's '. . . so you see things are not as black as they seem . . . behind the smoke beautiful things are being made . . . truly beautiful things like these aerodrome lenses . . . they stand for the tradition of English craftsmanship and skill . . . dress these men in Italian costumes and you might take them for Venetian glassworkers of the sixteenth century. . . .'

This, in full Depression! In retrospect, one has some difficulty in understanding how such establishment mystification could ever have been described as social consciousness, or how the English Left could have praised English documentaries to the skies. In the perspectives of the time, it's understandable: by contrast with Hollywood glamour and triviality, it was easy to confuse what documentary actually was with what it could be; it was reasonable to hope that any direction of attention towards real life might give real people a keener sense of their own worth and dignity, and make them more bolshy towards those who would exploit them. But, ominously, most of the films that resulted exactly fitted the establishment line of persuading people that everyone ought to feel happy and honoured just as they were.

And the tourist poetry of Flaherty's hear-no-evil, speak-no-evil, see-no-evil idyll is parodied almost word for word by Jacques Prévert in his script for *Les Amants de Vérone*, where Serge Reggiani, as a modern Venetian glassblower who knows that the work is gradually destroying his lungs, cynically repeats the unvarying pattern of a tourists' guide: '*ces modestes ouvriers qui semblent venir droit d'un tableau d'Uccello. . . .*'

To such dismal liberalism Franju's *En Passant par la Lorraine* is a quiet rejoinder. There is beauty, too, in the factory which Franju explores. But its beauty is that of a mechanical *Fleurs du Mal*. After a first viewing I had the impression of a film-within-a-film, that 'within the sponsor's film about Lorraine there existed Franju's film about a steelmill. The two are not rigidly separate . . . still, the two parts seemed too loosely linked for me to feel them as one.' At a second viewing they felt one.

Where *Le Sang des Bêtes* is a matter of ostentation leading to impregnation, in *En Passant par la Lorraine*, a minor film, impregnation leads to implication.

It has an archeological form, beginning with traces of the region's older strata and concluding with its contemporary *forces et voix*. After an array of stone Maids of Lorraine, it passes to a village fête recalling all the agreeable folklore of agricultural France. Amongst these 'amiable views' there are, to be sure, disquieting tones: the louring plains of Verdun, for example, whose sky is the colour, not of heroism, but of mud, and the camera's freezing on the face of the one child surviving from the massacre of Oradour, evoking certain territorial readjustments with France's neighbour. But the film moves steadily from the mediaeval-mythic to the agricultural-folkloric until it settles on an industrial complex which is a sinew of modern France.

The movement is not too obvious. The sequence opens, strikingly enough, with the flaming of coke-ovens, and then dwells on the slow passage of heavily-laden coke barges whose dumb-animal movement is a recurrent Franju motif. Then follows the clear, methodical revelation of steelmill procedure.

Steel production is one of those industrial processes which are the answer to the mediocre documentarist's prayer. It's almost impossible to avoid wowing an audience with the coursing

Still: En Passant par la Lorraine. *The Thomas Converter.*

streams of molten metal, the Brock's Benefit of sprayed sparks, the flames billowing from the orifices of converters, the human silhouettes in their ghoulish goggles, and so forth. But that is the rhetoric from which Franju abstains. This mill is grey, massive, unexcited; with immense, simple immovability, it contains all those processes within it. What another film-maker would whoop up lyrically, Franju reduces to repetitive processes. A stubby ingot is slid into a mould, from which it emerges thinned and lengthened into a white-hot worm, gripped and tipped over by hooks, and thrust again into the press, whence, each time, it emerges longer, thinner, eventually threadlike. The rhythms of the sequence are remorseless, but calm and solid, those of an obsessional torturing. Endowed as is this supple length with a luminous, fragile quality, almost of vivacity, and impregnated as it is with the dangerous energy of its heat, it acquires an extraordinary ambivalence which is only distorted by the tempting comparison to a snake. In this institution, steel becomes as soft and tender as putty: flesh, therefore. . . .? The workmen, rendered contemptuous (and sometimes careless) by long familiarity and easy mastery, snap off lengths of supple rod and then swing whirling lariats of white-hot steel over their shoulders. The price of their proud nonchalance is the accidents that must ensue.

Here Franju combines a clear elucidation of technique with a poetic accusation as trenchant as Hardy's description of the mechanical harvester in *Tess of the d'Urbervilles*. In its massive energy, its regular thrustings, its brutal caresses, the process takes on the quality of a monstrous, mechanical sexuality, which is incessant, insatiable, and untender. It takes on the quality of unremitting exploitation, of some sort of death-machine. The dwarfing of the human figures, the tracer-bullet-like pattern of the lariats, recall, occultly, wars, as if the only detumes-

cence of which our industrial Molochs are capable is the hideous *potlach* of war. Vigo, more obviously but no more effectively, tilted his camera to turn factory chimneys into cannon. Here Verdun and Oradour have already brought world wars near the surfaces of our minds. Not that industrialisation is the root of war (any more than money is the root of evil). We have already been reminded of Joan of Arc, who, as warrior, saint and maid, is a quite exceptionally militaristic figure.

We are returned to Lorraine, the factories squatting amongst the cornfields at dusk, the incessantly burning slagheaps, and the lanterns of the village fête, which fade away into the darkness, a darkness which suddenly evokes the ominously uncertain situation of human festivity and community in industrial routines.

Frame: plaster warrior in Hôtel des Invalides.

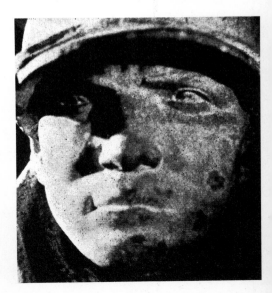

Hôtel des Invalides

Hôtel des Invalides is Franju's own favourite among his short films, possibly because it combines the subtlety of *En Passant par la Lorraine* with the denunciatory violence of *Le Sang des Bêtes*, and represents a more insolent subversion than either. In this misguided tour of the Hôtel des Invalides—which might be described as a combination of the Imperial War Museum and the Chelsea Hospital—the steelmill is replaced by a museum, the slaughtered beasts by only half-slaughtered men.

A ghostly Eiffel Tower fades wearily into a grey mist. Birds circle the funereal silhouettes of Paris monuments; their flight seems like an effort to escape reduced to the hopeless treading of an aerial treadmill.

The theme is crystallised as an old veteran is pushed in a wheelchair across the desolate courtyard. From then on, the monuments become protests against themselves. A damaged bronze bust becomes a slaughtered man; a half-suit of armour becomes a legless man. A priest officiates with style and grace while the disfigured faces of his congregation are silently revealed to the camera. The inscription 'Napoleon III, Roi de Rome', makes an apt comment on military vainglory. The film might have been dedicated to all those conscripts who fought in useless wars, the people about whom official rhetoric is silent, but who exist, unless one is prepared to argue that all wars have been justified.

A biplane suspended from the museum roof seems to 'machine-gun' three civilians passing in the courtyard beyond. In the (sparingly used) newsreel material, an officer looks at his watch; the time to go 'over the top' has come. This temporal specificity chimes poignantly with the museum context, and with that dreadful nostalgia so curiously inherent in World War I material. Has this nostalgia come about because, for us, it was grandfather's war, and sons so often forgive in their grandfathers the faults they accuse in their fathers? World War I was both archaic (with its cavalry spirit) and technological (with gas and flamethrowers); its machinery is quaint, yet the massed infantry make both the massiveness and the humanity hideously graspable. The effect of inverted nostalgia is given a new direction when a girl pauses by a mockup of the trenches of the Chemin des Dames and uses a periscope mirror to tidy her hair. It's both a bitter comment on the ephemerality of sacrifice, and a tribute to her absence of concern. But time's circle is completed as the singing schoolchildren leave the museum in their crocodiles, the cannon-fodder of tomorrow.

At its first and second viewing, the emotionally climactic shots take one's breath away. But such effects change with repetition. One says change rather than fade, for the memory of their earlier impact adheres to them, carrying an almost sacred aura of horror (for their content), gratitude (for their truth) and admiration (for Franju's aesthetic skill). Nonetheless, despite these accretions, the climaxes naturally lose their pristine impact. Now hitherto supporting shots emerge from the fading show of the climaxes, and reveal their finesse of mood, their quieter points. After five or six viewings, the film has turned inside out, the emotional peaks become the valleys, the valleys the peaks, one's initial response (horror, pity, indignation) has come to be amplified by something more complex, less definable, more musical in its intensity and evasiveness; a sense of tragic bewilderment, like the lucid helplessness of a nightmare.

'I asked Jarre to write a polka because it has a little 1900 streak which goes very well with the bronze head of that brave General Mangin which was knocked about by the Germans . . . at last, a mutilated man who didn't suffer. . . . He wouldn't have put a polka with a General's head if he hadn't been asked for it. In fact he asked me: "Don't you think it'll be too comic? . . ." ' But how jaunty does a polka have to be before it disrupts a scene instead of counterpointing it? What mysterious affinity can a polka and a bronze head possess that they call for each other, in the poet's mind, and then make sense, intuitively, even to those of us who would never have thought of such a conjunction and who, having experienced it, still can't account for it? Quite apart from questions of form or content, there is an aspect of film poetry, of all poetry, of all art, which has received scant

attention but is no less fundamental and extensive: that matter of tact, of a tactful tactlessness, of sensing dissonant conjunctions which can't be explained until the very terms of our thinking about human experience have been profoundly revised. Of all Franju's films, *Hôtel des Invalides* is perhaps the most intricate in its net of tact and anti-tact. Perhaps this is the reason why it's his favourite among his documentaries.

Stills: Hôtel des Invalides. *Left—the future interrogates the past. Below—*La Cour des Victoires. *Right—General Mangin.*

Le Grand Méliès, Monsieur et Madame Curie

As Franju remarked, violence and tenderness attract each other, like opposite poles; the violence of his slaughter triptych makes them his intensest films. But the temptation to see the minor documentaries as dilutions of the trio unleashed between 1949 and 1952 should be resisted. The quieter, minor films have their own quality, simply because they imbue ordinary, non-sensational, everyday reality with elegiac bitterness, with a kind of Surrealist stoicism. In the earlier films, the poetic synthesis is between violence and tenderness; in the minor films, it is between the humble-banal and the tragic-poetic.

In the first three films, savage subjects are seen with, not a savage, but a tender eye. Subsequently the tenderness which exists, so to speak, behind the camera, appears before the camera. It dawns, openly, in two biographical cameos, the first of Franju's films to centre on, and adopt the perspectives of, individual human beings.

These perspectives, and the subjects' connections with the vanished, pre-1914 world, naturally impel Franju away from the pure documentary to the reconstructed documentary, a semi-fictional format. Madame Curie is played by Nichole Stéphane, a choice hinting

at Franju's underlying affinities with that least documentary of film-makers, Jean Cocteau. In Jean-Pierre Melville's adaptation of *Les Enfants Terribles*, Nichole Stéphane played the domineering sister with an uncanny intensity which, in a more restrained key, informs Franju's film: 'As you can't photograph radioactivity, I decided to show the radioactivity in Nichole Stéphane's eyes.'

Both films, however, enclose their fiction episodes within a documentary structure. 'This story ends unhappily, so let us begin with the end and get the sad part over first', says the English version of the commentary of *Le Grand Méliès* (although in fact the film returns to the present at the end). Thus the fact of fictional reconstruction becomes meaningful, is poetically activated; what we are seeing is not even a memory, but only a well-meaning approximation. The overtones become even more poignant in that the film shows Madame Méliès herself, both in the past, playing Good Fairy in her husband's films, and in the present, a widow, still living in the 'home for retired actors' where

Frames: from the start of Le Grand Méliès. *Views of Home and Grounds; Madame Méliès visited by her son.*

her husband died. George Méliès, in the past, is played by his son, André; the two periods, the two planes, meet, when the son—ambiguously himself and his father—visits his mother and, sitting at the piano, plays the waltz which his dead father composed in his mother's honour. Franju himself knew Méliès and, indeed, brought him his last medicines. The separation-togetherness of a devoted couple, in time, is a strong counterpoint in the second film, which is called, not like the American film, *Madame Curie*, but *Monsieur et Madame Curie*. Pierre Curie dies long before their joint work

RARANTE ANS
PLUS TÔT...
AU THÉÂTRE
ROBERT-HOUDIN...

triumphs; his image 'freezes' into the stasis of memory. It's ironical that death should be suggested by perpetuating an image; but the irony is typical of the cinema whose continuity is an essentially Heraclitean flux; the cinema records the river's flowing, and the freezing of an image resembles the sudden fixity on the face of a corpse.

The wistful Pirandellism of *Le Grand Méliès* validates Franju's infidelity of detail, and even spirit. Madame Méliès spiritedly protested against Franju's legend that every week she visited her husband's grave and placed a bunch of violets on it ('he detested flowers!'). In interviews, Franju readily volunteers the information that the aged Méliès was very much more bitter than the film suggests. Franju links fact (Méliès was reduced to keeping a toyshop in the Gare Montparnasse) with the poetic iconography of the Prévert generation. Like the travelling toy and novelties salesman in the Préverts' *Adieu Léonard*, Méliès, as a toyshop keeper, becomes the custodian of the spirit of eternal youth, of magic, of poetry, and so has an immunity from the rancour of a businessman ruined by American pirates, by a world war, and by his own unadaptability. But Franju's Méliès is Méliès the artist, '*tel qu'en lui-même enfin l'éternité le change.*'

If *Le Grand Méliès* is a tribute to a showman's intuitive poetry, *Monsieur et Madame Curie* is a tribute to the scientific quest as poetry. It is also a pointed destruction of the Curie legend *à la* M.G.M., which treated Madame Curie as the St Joan of Arc of scientific progress, all shining grace and inspirations. Here, Madame Curie boils the pitchblende in a clumsy black pot in a frozen courtyard leading off a back alley; the Curies work with cheap apparatus in a smoke-besmirched laboratory. Usually considered a

Frames: Le Grand Méliès. *Conjuring with time.*

purely intellectual quest, their story here recaptures not simply its materialism, but the poetry of practicality, the sense of dirty, undignified *manual* labour, of lives lived through together, and apart, with none of the empty grandeur with which eventual success retrospectively veils the dirty hands, the frozen fingers, the limited horizons, the blind loyalty.

The culture-heroes of both films are associated with that pre-1914 era which must have cast its long shadows through Franju's childhood (especially in a rural district). The Proustian sense of time evolved from the film's constructions evokes the bitter-sweet pessimism of Max Ophuls, although Franju, unlike Ophuls, is not even *apparently* a romantic. But the comparison with Ophuls illuminates the films' flaw. Moving as their documentary aspects are, the dramatic reconstructions have a slight stiltedness which has been attributed to Franju's inexperience with actors or with human stories. Certainly documentarists are often poor or weak with actors, and Franju's way with actors derives more from a flair for personality than from his excelling as an 'actors' director'. But the stiltedness extends even to the lighting and composition of certain scenes—Méliès' 'shadowplay' with Lumière, the Curies

with their equipment—and this is so surprising, in the context of Franju's style, that I suspect there may have been a more sophisticated failure, to find, in the often parlous conditions of short film-making, the exact balance between the lived and the elegiac.

Franju's films, more, perhaps, than most (or more surprisingly than most, in view of their apparent homogeneity) change with successive viewings; and flaws which in any case are experienced as merely local become less conspicuous at each viewing; for they lie not in the conception of the films, but only in slightly awkward or tentative presentation.

Here, the stones of Paris weep for her distinguished sons. When the widowed Madame Méliès passes under the *art nouveau* grille of a Paris Métro station, and follows the black wall of the Père Lachaise cemetery it is as if she had stepped past the elan of her youth, itself a metallic fossil, into the long, hard blackness of solitude. And the bunch of violets which she takes down into the Métro is the only soft flower-form in the tiled tunnels of a labyrinthine underworld.

Frames: the world created by Georges Méliès in his studio.

Les Poussières, Navigation Marchande

With *Les Poussières* Franju reverts to the harshly accusatory tone of *Le Sang des Bêtes*. Franju was asked to make a film which would (1) encourage industrial workers to be constantly on their guard against the danger posed to their health and efficiency by industrial dust, and (2) stress the efficacy of routine precautionary methods. Franju reasoned that if you have to make a film urging workers to be constantly vigilant, then routine precautions aren't sufficient. (A point with wider implications: when workers want to infuriate management, they work to rule. Why are the rules such an obstacle to work? So that management can disclaim responsibility for disasters by saying the worker should have observed the rule. But at the same time, the worker dare not observe the rule!) Thus Franju's film on safety becomes a film about danger.

The invisible scourge is actualised for the camera by microscopic photography and by examples of its diffusion of light, and by shots

Frames: Le Grand Méliès. *Madame Méliès takes a bunch of violets to her husband's grave. Flowers, and the gently curving forms of hair and art nouveau, evoke the timelessness of youth in a stony world.*

of trees killed and petrified by the dust which the workmen breathe into their lungs. Over a shot of a smiling workman Franju superimposes his chest X-ray and over that the medical phrase: 'a snowstorm of nodules of silicosis'. Silicosis, though incurable, crippling and often fatal, is not recognised as an industrial disease by the French Social Security. So much for precautions! (According to Gabriel Vialle, the sponsors of *Les Poussières*, L'Institut National de Sécurité, subsequently commissioned a short on industrial medicine from Resnais; what he gave them (*Le Mystère de l'Atelier Quinze*) was a denunciation of the working conditions in most factories!) There is a chilling contrast between the white, pure ethereality of Limoges porcelain and the ravages wreaked on the craftsmen's lungs.

The film begins by evoking sidereal dust and concludes with radioactive dust. Industry is only a link in the great chain of natural processes.

Navigation Marchande was sponsored by a French steamship line, and its producers asked Franju to show (1) the fitting-out of their ships, and (2) to 'show people guzzling in a first-class dining room', as he put it. Franju was agreeable enough about the first point, though rather dubious as to the artistic interest of the second. Instead, he found a maritime establishment whose chapel was convertible into a ballroom—in a few moments, the altar could be converted into a bar, and the genuflections of the faithful into the lively steps of the tango. Franju was enchanted by this physical illustration of the Janus face of Western culture. Unfortunately, his producers got wind of his intentions, and telephoned the steamship line's publicity officer, who, like the good guy in a B Western, turned up just in time to foil the devilish schemes of the bad guy (Franju). Franju isn't very interested in the film, though passages have a sombre poetry.

A Propos d'une Rivière, Mon Chien

The film first titled *Le Saumon Atlantique* was subsequently renamed *Au Fil de la Rivière* or *A Propos d'une Rivière*, which evoke leisure, holidays, a certain poetry, and other forms of agreeable human interest. Shooting was somewhat upset by the fact that the river chosen as location, on the strength of its reputation for positively pullulating with salmon, obstinately refused to yield a single example of the species; a few fish had to be imported, and recourse was finally made to stock shots taken from a Spanish newsreel. The exasperation evoked in Franju by the film is nicely summed up by his anecdote: 'I don't mind telling you that while I was shooting the scene with the salmon on the end of the line, I got so mad I was kicking that salmon up the arse—he kept going out of shot, the cunt. They said, "Don't keep kicking him, he'll go white." He was pulling so hard on the line that in the end he went off like a torpedo!'

Franju's anecdote may shock some as much as the fact that the donkey, which, in Buñuel's *Terre sans Pain* allegedly loses its footing and slips to its death, actually falls because Buñuel had it shot—Kyrou remarks that the puff of smoke from the rifle is visible on the screen. Bu no-one who eats fish can object to such 'cruelty', and it's true that donkeys really do

56

miss their footing on those paths. Indeed, the violence in Franju's account of his intervention confirms his 'If I make a film about salmon I don't give a hang for the fisherman, all that interests me is the salmon.'

It's in the same spirit that this remark completely misrepresents the form of the film. Apparently written at the last moment, in response to the evasiveness of fish, the script centres on an old man, lamenting the scarcity of salmon in these streams, and remembering how, as a youngster, he would slip off from school and fish alone. The images of his halcyon days glow with summer's high glare and rich shadows; the boy's truant world is rich and ripe with freedom. Then he remembers his prime, and we see him, in waders and beret, with mean mouth and teeth, an epitome of rural spite. As an old man, his blend of picturesqueness and mediocrity results in the pathos of nothingness. Franju's calm juxtaposition of these contradictions has the quality of a double riddle. It reverts to the theme of time's paradoxes from *Le Grand Méliès*, though these are puzzles of personality rather than of fortune. And it prefigures the 'riddle' in *Thérèse Desqueyroux*, where Edith Scob enjoys nothing more than banging away with shotguns at birds, and fingers the little bundles of flesh and feathers in her hands before strangling them.

Every year, when Parisian families leave for the long summer holidays, thousands of pets are abandoned, or stray from their provisional homes. *Mon Chien* is the story of one such pet. Paterfamilias abandons him while driving the family down to the Côte d'Azur. The dog resourcefully finds his way back to their Parisian home, and, roaming the streets, fends for himself, pending their return. But he is picked up by the municipal authorities, who dispose of unreclaimed pets in their gas chambers.

Critics sometimes like to believe that as enlightened onlookers they see most of the game, and that, by taking their advice, the artist can improve his strokes and strategy, even, perhaps, improve his contact with the real sources of his inspiration. There's a little truth in this, or at least, a potentiality of truth. In so far as we critics are, in Elia Kazan's words, 'eunuchs in a harem', who would wish to deny us our consoling illusions? But if the good critic ever helps an artist, it is probably in a different way: his response is symptomatic of a certain stratum of opinion, and if that is the stratum at which the artist aims, the critic is, so to speak, a flag signalling, not only *that*, but *in which direction* the shot went wide. Sometimes the critic can be an artist about the artist, but his hypotheses about the artist's spiritual processes are usually more useful to his readers than to the artist, simply because reconstructing the precise steps and the profound motivations of an artist's thought implies not only an exceptionally rare knowledge of the actual situation in which the artist found himself but an almost sinister degree of spiritual empathy. If

Still: the young truant from A Propos d'une Rivière.

such empathy is often taken for granted, it's partly because megalomania is a critic's occupational disease, but partly because current sentimentality about Communication presents it as an exchange of precise X-ray plates rather than as the far less precise and analytical, and indeed extremely ambiguous and overdetermined, affair of appeal and response.

Since the film director must constantly re-adapt to financial, physical or metereological circumstances, and the special talents and personalities of his collaborators, it often happens that the director himself is a far more enlight-ened critic of his own work than a critic can be, and it always happens that he can contribute something which critics can't. (For this reason, as well as for the primitive condition of film criticism, the interviewing of artists looms larger in film criticism than in literary criticism.) Not that directors can always remember or analyse at the time specifically *which* possibili-

Frame: Mon Chien. *An image that might be a symbol for the animal kingdom—increasingly at the untender mercies of the naked ape.*

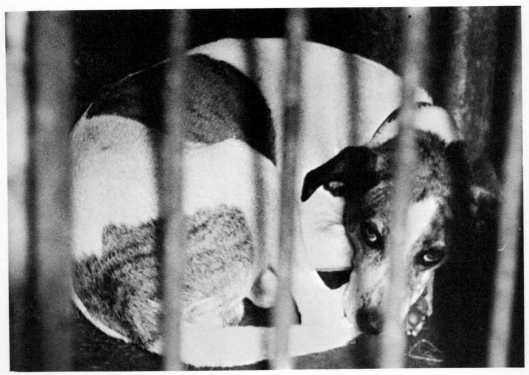

ties came into their mind, only to be regretfully, or mistakenly, left alone; but if they can be induced to speak frankly (which rarely happens), their hindsight has a special value.

It could seem that *Mon Chien* was, in its way, a children's film like *Bim*, also written by Prévert; or that Franju's bleak style, less emphatic here than in earlier movies, provided an adequate counterpoint to a necessarily rather sentimental story. Franju feels 'I should have shown only one victim—the girl as well was too much.' And he suffered from a failure of nerve. 'But I backed down. I reckoned that even if I did show the dogs being gassed, it would only be cut out anyway. Cut or not, I should still have filmed it.'

The film's criticism is, of course, directed against the families who abandon their pets, not against the authorities who establish the gaschambers. The object of the artist's protest is not so much the system, but the individuals for whom animals are merely toys, to be junked like toys when their novelty palls. But if you don't respect the life-force in other living things, you don't respect it in yourself. The formulation links with an inconspicuous, but profound, trait in Franju's feature films. Most of the brutality shown by the villains is secondary to a subdued joylessness; their constant egoism is an aspect of their insensibility. The principal exceptions are the doctors, in the first two features, who play God. But even Genessier's pompous walk has a kind of soft deadness, even his megalomania can be seen as a rigid defence against the fact that he's a two-legged animal kept in some internal cage.

If *Mon Chien* may seem insufficiently rigorous in its compassion, by the higher standards (and it's in no sense *Lassie Come Home*), its prefiguration of *Au Hasard Balthasar* underlines those curious affinities between Franju and Bresson which both, perhaps, would like to repudiate. Like Bresson, Franju knows the 'sound of silence', the eerie familiarity of isolated sounds like the raking of gravel, the mystery of the inexpressive face, the monotone. Both their styles relate to a bleak loneliness. Both remain deliberately exterior to any psychological analysis, and the loose dramatic articulation of *Thérèse Desqueyroux* recalls Bresson's. It's possible to imagine a Franju version of *Journal d'un Curé de Campagne*, and how subtle would be the changes needed to transform its shooting script from an indication of spiritual values, however invisible, into a tragedy of their sensed, but denied, inexistence.

Le T.N.P., Sur le Pont d'Avignon

'In the film I've made about the Théâtre National Populaire, I naturally took great care to avoid the pitfall of "filmed theatre". But I had to keep the "theatre" and by resorting to documentary artifices I think I achieved "theatrical cinema". . . . In a scene at Genevilliers, we see the actors in their dressing rooms intercut with the emptying of coke-ovens. The last shot shows Sylvia Montfort as she's called on stage. She's in a court dress. She looks in a mirror. The image dissolves into the immense curtain rising . . . not on the play, but a viaduct out in the country. Over the viaduct passes the

Flèche d'Or. Revealed like this, it takes on a glittering life. . . .' Such cutting is more than merely 'detheatricalisation' by exercises in Eisensteinian montage—or arbitrary cutaways hoping to be taken for Eisensteinian montage. This construction makes Franju's film a series of confrontations, or rather connections, between the world of the theatre, the world in the theatre, and the world. And the connections make a special point. The arts are often thought of as a window on the world, justified for their widening of our sensibility's horizons. As often as not they become, in practice, merely a mirror for a class or a coterie, a rejection of any wider reality. By its foundation statutes, the T.N.P. is required, not only to perform in its Parisian theatres, but to tour France and play to popular audiences.

The film is a model of non-narrative structure. An early shot establishes that the people queuing for tickets at the T.N.P. are more proletarian than the typical theatre crowd; but the statement is so quiet it is almost subliminal. A few shots later, an actor in period costume emerges from the Stage Door and, smoking, gazes at the black chimneys that tower over him from a nearby factory. His face is not quite expressionless, there is a quiet recognition of those factories, a recognition as tough as that of a warrior for his adversary, as gentle as that of a man for the men who work in them. His smoke and theirs establishes an affinity of tension. Jean Vilar, sitting alone amongst the auditorium's empty seats critically watching a rehearsal, becomes the *representative* of the audience (an attitude which would distress all those who so resent any mention of The Masses in film criticism). The curtain rises on a tour of the world, but it's not a tourist's world. The capitals of the world remain postcards in an album, which is all they are, and cinematic movement is kept for factories, for trains, for ships, for the workaday world, which reveals its 'glittering life'. The scenes of dressing-room tension are nothing to do with stage-fright; between reality and the other reality which is reached through illusion lies a 'zone' in which the actors are uneasy, which can be traversed only by technique and discipline. Monique Chaumette, rehearsing in streetclothes, gives her cue to Maria Casarès, who replies during a performance, in costume, from which Franju cuts to a liner leaving the port of Marseilles. Time, as in *Le Grand Méliès*, and space, as in *Le Sang des Bêtes*, are interwoven, as are art's passionate splendour and reality's brooding nostalgia. The film reaches a climax on the merger of all these worlds: Maria Casarès in the sleepwalking scene from *Macbeth*, a scene which, among other things, achieves a perfect fusion of all the problems involved in filmed theatre. In the dark stage, we see only lights and faces. Space is both active visually, and abstract in setting. Thus there is no conflict between its theatrical and cinematographic existence. As in the theatre, nothing competes with the actor's presence. Franju so cuts between longshot and close-up as perfectly to conjugate cinematic intimacy and theatrical intensity. For the English spectator, the Pirandellism gets an extra dimension, by one of those happy chances which only happen to works of art which deserve it (less mystically, which reach sufficient intensity to stimulate the spectator's mind into gratefully reinterpreting the happy accident): one is listening to Shakespeare in French, and translating back. The scene chosen is a sleepwalking scene; a scene of deep feelings emerging through hallucination and dream, which is what art is too. The world in art is as tense, as criminal, as black as that of the factory chimneys.

Franju reverses that currently popular Pirandellism whereby, if art and life resemble each other, this must prove that life is an unreal illusion. For Franju as for the Surrealists, art is a sector of life, and as real, and as lived. What we create isn't unreal, and the belief that reality is illusion is the most desperate of all illusions.

Anticipating two weeks in July to spare while waiting for the T.N.P. in Avignon, and with a film crew on hand, Franju quickly prepared an ironic little film to be made in the interval. An apt comment on the tourist's eye occurs when Franju fills the colour, CinemaScope, movie screen with black-and-white postcards of Avignon monuments. But he got a surprise; in colour and 'Scope, the black-and-white post-cards took on an unsuspected relief, and became quite interesting. Franju cherishes one of the film's subversive side-effects. The local authorities had decided to suppress the usual 14 July fireworks to honour those who had died in Indochina. But when they heard that a film was

Still: the sleep-walking scene from Le T.N.P.

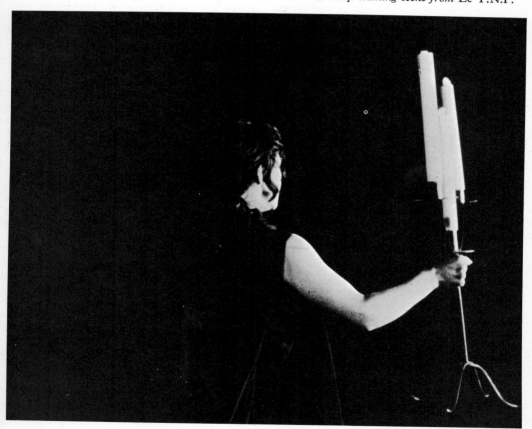

being made which would present Avignon to the great world of potential tourists, the hitherto grief-stricken city did a quick turnabout and mounted an unusually magnificent display. So much for the glorious dead.

The film reverses the proposition of the T.N.P. There the illusion, and the real, encounter and reaffirm each other. The spiritual becomes concrete. Here the concrete reveals itself as an illusion. Tourist Avignon is as empty of spiritual meaning as the Palais des Papes, as two-dimensional as a postcard, as false as fireworks at a funeral.

Notre Dame, Cathédrale de Paris

The film takes as its text Le Corbusier's evocation of the days 'when the cathedrals were white'. The quotation from a fellow-travelling, rationalist functionalist states the key in which the film moves. In colour and Dyaliscope, it translates sensitively to the screen the shapes, rhythms, volumes and mass of what is not so much a cathedral as a structure in stone. It agnosticizes it; and since the cathedral has also lost its organic position as a social focus, it squats in Paris as sad a derelict as the table and chandelier of Le Sang des Bêtes. Symbols of its impotent malevolence, acid-gnawn gargoyles

haul themselves out of the smirched stone and pull faces at the blue, haze-bound city. Pigeons fly against the bells, and stun themselves, or die of cold on the parapet. (His eye is no more on the sparrow than on the lamb.) The camera moves to the great doorway and penetrates it, embarking on its journey to the interior. The red cardinals' hats hang under the roof, floating in mid-air, turning slowly in the penumbra like jellyfish in submarine currents, throwing a purple glow on the walls. While a nun begs alms for the poor, the camera dwells on the costly gold pieces which exemplify the Roman Catholic Church's own peculiar brand of wordly vanity. (If this anticlerical gibe is a hoarily traditional one it is because it is hoarily relevant; Buñuel makes the same point in *Terre Sans Pain*.) Under the solemn, sad, dead spaces of the lofty stone, the tracking camera reveals ranks and files of empty chairs, like the skeletal backbone of some prehistoric monster; Roger Tailleur speaks of 'Ionesco's chairs in the nave of Notre-Dame'. Notre Dame, a white elephant, as enigmatic already as Stonehenge.

A pious spectator remarked to Franju's wife: 'Ah, Madame Franju, allow me to shake your hand. I saw your husband's film about Notre Dame, how beautiful! and then all those empty chairs, ah! Madame, one can sense that Monsieur Franju is a devout Catholic, one understands that he is saying, "Look at those seats! where thousands of believers will come to pray." '

'For *Notre Dame*, I told myself: I'll be shooting in December, I'll have bad weather. But actually I don't know what I'll have, so once again I'll have to accommodate the unforeseeable. . . . It so happens that if you're given a month like December, you don't have mist the whole month, you don't have sunshine the whole month and you don't have snow all the time either. . . . So the film is in three parts. The towers are in sunshine. From the height of

62

the towers, we look out over Paris in mist. We go inside and when we come out for the last time Paris is in snow. It's very lovely.'

These inconspicuous foreshortenings of weather recall the jugglings with time and reality-illusion in *Le Grand Méliès* and *Le T.N.P.* The effect isn't to contrast the monumental immutability of Mother Church (or even of an ignoble pile) with 'time like an ever-rolling stream'. The cathedral's peace is not just that of its death; like the good God, it never was alive.

La Première Nuit

Frames: from La Première Nuit. *Public and private sectors . . .*

'It needs only a little imagination for our most habitual actions to become charged with a disquieting significance, for the decor of our daily life to give birth to a fantastic world.' So runs the introduction with which Franju furnished *La Première Nuit*, in order to alert and attune the audience to savour the shift from reality to fantasy for its own sake. Not that the film has no dramatic or social content, still less is it simply an exercise in gear-changing between moods. But the dramatic charge is concentrated in the *fact* of changing.

There may well have been a supplementary,

and more mundane, reason for the title. Most of the movies in the French supporting short slot are pretty dreary documentaries, and many audiences, after blunting the film's imagination with their own expectations, would have wasted the first part of the film readjusting. Even then, they might expect this to be a dramatic film, and while waiting for the story to 'get going', fail to attend to the details of mood.

A little boy who is usually taken to school by

Frames: La Première Nuit. *The map is not the territory; but it is a territory . . .*

chauffeur-driven car escapes, and spends a night down in a Métro station, alone, dreaming about a little girl whom he glimpsed during the day. He dreams that he rides, alone, in a subway car. As it runs parallel alongside another train, he sees through the double layer of windows the girl, also alone. They stare at each other silently; as the trains run side by side, first one gaining a little, then the other, their swaying is as of a waltz—a waltz in eerily empty boxes of glass and steel hurtling on their rigidly predestined rails. Then the trains move apart, and curve away, and the moments of their magic encounter are gone. The boy lies curled up on the lower step of a static escalator; and as the station staff return, and the workaday current flows again, the escalator moves, lifting him back to reality.

Nonetheless, the film is called: *La Première Nuit*. Perhaps it's only a first encounter: an initiation, sexual certainly, social possibly. The poor little rich boy has escaped from his cosy, stifling, chauffeured world, and found the path to the freedom of dreams. But the film is also pessimistic, or, at least, not yet optimistic. For those dream trains don't run in reality. And they're empty trains, trains as lonely as outer space, as orbiting asteroids. Let's hope, though, that the boy becomes a confirmed truant, keeps slipping away from home and school, until, in the end, his dreamtime can synchronize with the city's day. But that's an even longer journey; one on which most sensitive people lose their way, becoming, for example, *merely* poets.

Not that this is a moralising film; or rather, the moral is implicit in the mixture of innocence and sadness, or precocity and defeat. Dreams are woven out of the relative speeds with which steel carriages hurl themselves through their labyrinthine grave (and perhaps it's those very same trains which at last come rumbling out into the sad grey day, near the mortuary of *Les Yeux sans Visage*).

Franju's sense of space, place and pace is so precise that the movement of the trains acquires an extraordinary ambivalence, unmatched even by the slow advance of the tanks in Pabst's *Westfront* 1918. The trains seem at once to ram themselves into the stations, and to drag themselves away, as they slew past the camera. As they slant off on their separating gradients, their movement seems that of birds banking, or,

Frames: La Première Nuit. *The trains' dance.*

more accurately perhaps, of strange flying insects, machine-insects.

Gabriel Vialle takes a shot from the film as an example of Franju's consistent resort to movement within the shot (as Bazin noted of Wyler) rather than of cutting between the elements, 'in this case, the inspector going by on his bicycle, on his last rounds, so as to mark the transition to the dilated time-sense of the dream. Moreover, to movement in the shot is added shifts of focus, and by the clarity of different fields in depth, Franju draws our attention to: first, the hero of the film, then the new character entering into the shot and, again, the hero. This movement, in depth, gives to the movement in the shot a supplementary dimension which is situated elsewhere, on two levels of significance. On the material level, our attention is solicited not only by a lateral movement but by a double movement from foreground to background, from background to foreground. On the psychological level, the result of these procedures is to create a new universe—the dream-like vision of a very familiar daily reality.'

If there is a flaw in the film's spell, it lies in the acting; perhaps the most difficult of all moods for child actors to grasp is that intent somnambulism, that quality of blind listening, that mediumistic alertness of these dreamed dreamers. Yet, at a second and third viewing, this film, like all of Franju's, like the poems of any authentic poet, seem to adapt themselves to their flaws. This isn't to claim that the flaws themselves have meaning (if they do, they're not really flaws, it is the critic who misinterpreted them in the first place). And one should, as far as one can, distinguish between style as statement and style as symptom. But the film survives its flaw as interestingly as a beautiful face can survive a scar. And when a face is familiar, who sees the scars?

The point is worth labouring a little, for most

of Franju's films are flawed (as most of Jean Renoir's are flawed), and it's very easy for film critics to judge a film by its flaws rather than by its finesses, about which they maintain a resolute scepticism. The source of their insensitivity isn't far to seek. It lies in that still-prevalent assumption that films are only a minor art, or a very primitive art, or an art that one turns to only for relaxation (as if one couldn't relax in the presence of subtlety), or that an art of images must somehow be devoid of nuance. No wonder that the most fervent despisers of the cinema flock to absorb the gospel according to McLuhan, with its comforting message that in the electric media the content doesn't matter, that the medium is the message, that one film is much like another film, that, in short, the cinema isn't a culture at all, and that those who think it is are the victims of an amiable obsession. It must be very hard for those who pride themselves on their culture to admit to themselves that a mere film director, a denizen of show-business, can be too subtle for them, can be visually more literate, discerning and refined, can be sharper and more devious in his response to formal intricacy and spiritual implication.

Frames: La Première Nuit. *End of an encounter.*

La Tête contre les Murs

François Gérane (Jean-Pierre Mocky) is a delinquent adolescent from an upper middle-class home. Impelled by some obscure torment, he blames his father for his mother's death, declasses himself, sports a leather jacket and rides his motor-cycle obsessively, endangering his own, and others', life and limb. He breaks into his father's office, steals some money and wantonly burns a pile of papers from an important legal brief. This last act, bringing him no advantage, reveals that his sadism against his father has a *visionary* quality, and, accordingly, he seems insane. The father, marked by that logical severity which is more apparent in the French than in the English bourgeoisie, is unwilling to send this waster to prison, less through paternal forbearance than through anxiety to avoid a scandal. For those who are certified insane don't get reported, or even tried.

Policy at the asylum is something of a stalemate between two viewpoints. Dr Valmont (Pierre Brasseur) is the champion of the 'old' school, for whom all subtlety is mere mystification; if a man's conduct isn't rational he's insane, if he's criminal he ought to be locked up, and if like Gérane he's irrational and criminal then vigilance is the most important consideration. Valmont's younger colleague, Dr Emery (Paul Meurisse) is more progressive, but Gérane's attempts to be transferred to his care provoke and fall foul of staff vanities and politics. He escapes, finds a job in Paris, where he is hidden by his girlfriend Stéphanie (Anouk Amée), a girl who, in her smoothly silent way is as aloof and mysterious as he is himself. Rather than involve her, he quits her, is recaptured and returned to the asylum, in whose terrifying atmosphere he will undoubtedly deteriorate and from which he may never emerge.

La Tête contre les Murs suffers from some discrepancies within its conception, and even more from the misunderstandings to which they give rise. It is based on a novel whose author dated it specifically in 1934, two years before the advent of new drugs began diminishing the reliance on crude forms of restraint (chains) and when public and medical attitudes to mental instability were rather more defensively vindictive than they are now. The faintly anachronistic air of the film's emphasis on incarceration gives those who need to believe that our society represents the best of all financially practicable worlds the chance to object that 'things aren't like that now'. And the public's fearful uncertainties about where sanity leaves off and insanity begins lend plausibility to the reassuring belief that doctors never make mistaken diagnoses. Also, various violent details may persuade some spectators that this is an unreliably 'sensational' film.

Furthermore before it was a Franju film, *La Tête contre les Murs* was set to be made by Jean-Pierre Mocky, who went on to become an intelligent and subversive director with a style totally opposed to Franju's. 'In 1956 I did an adaptation . . . I suggested it to several producers, even the Public Health were interested in it. They thought of it as a propaganda piece. I wrote the scenario with the idea of playing the epileptic [played in the film by Charles Aznavour—his first major screen part]. Charles Vanel and Fernand Gravey were to be the doctors, with Daniel Gelin in the lead. But there remained the problem of finding a director . . . in view of my tender years, the distributors refused me the chance to direct . . . Dassin was busy on *Celui qui doit Mourir*, Camus had just shot *Mort en Fraude* and didn't want to do another drama . . . I showed the shooting script to Resnais, who was more interested in the nurse than in the patient. I was getting nowhere. Then I met a journalist from Angers at a cocktail party given for the book's nth million. And just a I was about to give up, the journalist asked me the question which started everything off again: "Who do you want to direct?" On the spur of the moment I replied: "Franju". Franju met Bazin and they came to an agreement. Brasseur and Meurisse replaced Vanel and Gravey, Aznavour took the role I'd written for myself and I replaced Gelin. We asked Prévert to do the dialogue, but he wanted eight million francs and took too long to deliver. Sigurd didn't like the subject and turned it down. *In extremis*, Jean-Charles Pichon took it on. Bad weather complicated the shooting; with all these difficulties, we overshot the twenty million franc budget . . .'

It's not unusual for a subject to undergo such vicissitudes, even metamorphoses, and yet emerge as an integral whole. Indeed, the stamp of Franju's own style is on every shot. But the script isn't Franju's, and the visual style seems to conceal rather than highlight the structure, and the meanings in its structure. One can imagine Gelin's Gérane as possessing a sensitive charm lacking in Mocky's performance; and the films which Mocky himself went on to direct afford innumerable examples of ways in which such charm, far from being a matter of compromise, might be combined with quite mercurial powers of provocation. It is possibly

Franju, the director, rather than Mocky, the actor, who keys Gérane to a stolid, subdued style which, though utterly authentic, seems to oppose, rather than inveigle, the spectator's sympathies and insights. Dramatically speaking, too, there is a curious shift of interest between Gérane and the epileptic. Epilepsy, affecting a man of Mocky's solidity, might well have been more disturbing than epilepsy striking a man of Aznavour's frailty. As it is, the two characters seem insufficiently distinct: on the level of the script, one seeks freedom, and the other human contact, but Franju's representation through Gérane of the possibilities of, and need for, contact is so tight-lipped that the two characters almost become a tautology.

Certain fashionable conventions also further misunderstandings. Given such forerunners as *The Wild One* and *Rebel Without a Cause*, and widespread discussion of *les blousons noirs*, any leather-jacketed ton-up boy has only to appear, let alone attack his father in the name of his mother, to set the audience expecting the analysis of a neurosis. It may overlap, perhaps, with counter-accusations of society, as in both Benedek's and Ray's films, but will exist, nonetheless, on an expository, individual level. And this is precisely what Franju's film doesn't provide. The confrontation of father and son is psychologically schematic and not developed; its real function is to present a social climate. Ironically, the audience's expectations are furthered by a very beautiful scene which Franju added to the script and which, apart from its atmospheric interest, may have been intended to steer the audience's interest away from dramatic analysis to lyrical climates: Gérane, steering his machine across hilly country. But it comes at the opening, and many films open with such a lyrical piece before getting down to the story. And, in fact, the film subsequently hesitates between being (1) Gérane's story, (2) a lyrical piece about insanity and its depressions, and (3) a denunciation of certain social structures and the assumptions underlying them.

Furthermore, the lyricism itself is somewhat limited in range—limited to the obsessional-depressive which is the climate of Franju's style. Dramatically, this is perfectly legitimate in so far as it is Gérane's own key, and we are, in effect, seeing everything through his eyes. But the link with his subjectivity is somewhat obscured both by the shift of emphasis from Gérane in himself to the general processes of the asylum and by the blend of overwhelming poignancy in the long-shots, with a rather deadpan quality in the close-ups of the central characters.

The characterization, similarly, is rather a collage of Mocky's intelligently nuanced fictional icons, and of vignettes based on Franju's documentary experience. Franju's tense but deadpan stylistic restraint combats the sentimental possibilities of the icons, facilitates their integration with the minor characters, and reconciles both with the film's generally impersonal structure. The result is occasionally awkward, in that Mocky's, indeed everybody's, psychology seems to be somewhat arbitrary in its development. Gérane's inner battle against his darker side is somewhat forgotten in the course of his attempts to gain his freedom. The taut, gloomy, troubled attractiveness of the girl who could save him is a welcome change from the obvious sweetness-and-light figures, but she, too, remains something of a fascinating oyster. One or two of the vignettes (like the senior officer who sings patriotic songs) are doubtless justifiable, but, in the context of faintly arbitrary development, smack slightly of ideological *Schadenfreude*.

Superficially, at least, the film exists in a no-man's-land between the dramatic and the atmospheric. As Franju says: 'I admit I'm much more sensitive to the scenic than to the dynamic.

When I was tiny I saw a fire for the first time, and afterwards I saw the façade with nothing behind it. I've kept the vision of something very artificial and strange—a façade with nothing behind. And what was in front of it? Space—now haunted . . .'. The dynamism of Gérane's story is dramatic rather than scenic, and in his first feature Franju hasn't solved, as he was shortly to do, the difficulties of relating his scenic style to the dynamics of the script. Moreover, this script is conceived in the conventional, though honourable, terms of sympathy and shock which Franju's visionary style defeats. Franju evades rather than solves the problems by conceiving it as a film of atmosphere. It succeeds if the horror attains a quality of poetic fantasy.

Where the film dissatisfies, or arouses unsatisfied expectations, it does so for highly sophisticated aesthetic reasons. And inaccurate, incoherent, gawky, misunderstood as it may be on certain levels, it's not a film to be forgotten, still less ignored, even on those levels. Its accusation of 'the system' does retain an uncomfortable degree of reality, and it's worth insisting that it was made before the recent upthrust of concern about the climate of mental hospitals.

Naturally, the bureaucracy will flourish photographs of the latest hospitals, all white and bright in the sunlight, and assure us that those bleak, grim old buildings are in the process of being renovated. But 'in the process' means: 'many will still be the same for another fifty years'. As Franju says: 'I shot *La Tête* in the Psychiatric Hospital of Dury, with a quite unbelievable courtyard. Dead in the centre is a phallic tree with four benches grouped around it. Around the benches there are tulips and round the tulips there are high walls. The patients sit on the benches and all day long they look at the tree. I must admit I wouldn't have dared ask an art director for anything quite so "artificial", so demented, as that.'

'I insisted on shooting in an actual mental hospital so that everyone would be in the atmosphere. We were in it for six weeks, and it comes over in the film. Cameramen, technicians, actors, we all lived as a community in their community. We hardly emerged from it. We returned to Paris on Saturdays . . . we stayed in a hotel, and incidentally if we'd slept in the asylum, we'd still be there.' The atmosphere was so oppressive that on their first visit Anouk and Schuftan were in tears, and, in the course of shooting, Franju had to take to his bed for a few days.

'There's this dimension of bourgeois strangeness. It hasn't the picturesqueness of prison. That would be too simple, not so cruel. In a prison, there are bars, it's dank. A psychiatric hospital is quite different. It's the pavilion system with bungalows and gardeners galore . . . They cultivate tulips, but behind the tulips there are walls. And they're impassable, those walls behind the tulips. That's what's really revolting . . . there are espaliers on the walls, all

Still: outside the walls. Anouk Aimée in La Tête contre les Murs.

71

done to reassure the inmate; and that's worse than prison, stark and simple . . .'

Michael Parsy (interviewer): 'Aznavour, sitting by a small pond, speaks of the sea. Did you ever look for an asylum that was beside the sea?'

'I looked for one. It would have been worse. The sea's there, yet you can't bathe . . . It's very Surreal, the whole thing. It's so hideous because it's false: the tulips die, so they plant new ones. Everything has that sweet, flattering quality that's really monstrous.'

Jean Curtelin (interviewer): 'Personally, I find the Meurisse character far more monstrous

Still: La Tête contre les Murs: *the obsessional circles of the gambling club.*

than Brasseur . . .'

'Of course. There's a very characteristic scene, the one where Meurisse says: "Here, you have the bar, music, gay colours." I'll say it's gay . . . the traditionalist doctor is almost less revolting than the other. You know he's traditionalist. With the other fellow, it's "Sport, my lads, the bar!" '

The film leaves us in no doubt. Gérane strays into a sort of twilight area, bordering on the psychopathic (on his motorbike he nearly goes over a child, he threatens an old woman). He moves in a sort of twilight area between sanity and madness. He's sane and mad in parts: in other words, he's not 'mad'. He is caught in all the paradoxes besetting those whose protests are sprung by an alliance of confused decency and profound neurosis. His need for treatment is an aspect of a more basic need, a need for those who, for reasons of their own, can clarify the decency, direct the protest, and tolerate the neurosis. It might well turn out that by and large he's less neurotic than his father. But Valmont, understanding the sufferings of Gérane *père*, and refusing to understand the sufferings of Gérane *fils*—because of their socially nonconformist form—classifies him as mad. And the supposedly enlightened Dr Emery agrees. Certainly, his methods are more enlightened, more humane, more likely to be successful; but he is, in a profound sense, Valmont's accomplice. Will his criterion for sanity turn out to be anything other than 'sport, my lads, the bar!'?

But it may be suspected that only in melodramas are mental hospitals so badly run that the merely neurotic can land themselves in for long terms of imprisonment. This proposition is as pathetically naive as the belief that the law never errs. David Cooper quotes the case of a patient, who, after being dismissed from a mental hospital, was readmitted 'on a Detention Order (that is to say, a form of certification under the Mental Health Act of 1959 which removes from the patient his rights to leave hospital of his own accord, and, if he does so, provides for his forcible return to hospital by either police or hospital staff). The story was that this young man had, among other things which remained unspecified, behaved aggressively and violently towards his parents, and that he, as the order stated, had to be removed for the protection of others to an institution for observation of his mental state. His parents had referred their problem to the general practitioner who, with the assistance of the Mental Welfare Officer, had issued the Detention Order. However, when one probed deeply enough into the circumstances of the family crisis, one discovered that the aggressive and violent behaviour consisted in (a) breaking one tea cup, (b) slamming the front door, and (c) stamping his foot once, but rather emphatically, on the garden path.'

As John Gardner points out, 'for the patient who is alleged to be "mentally ill" . . . the ancient basic right of *habeas corpus* does not in practice apply. . . . There are authenticated cases in Massachusetts of nearly lifelong imprisonment in state mental institutions of persons who got lost in the works, so to speak, though they are normal enough to have been released from the beginning. The poor, the friendless loner, those who do not speak English, are all apt to be detained permanently, once they are admitted for any reason . . .'. The efficiency of the selection process is well rendered by the *Evergreen Review* editor, Seymour Krim, explaining how, in the summer of 1955, after an outburst of offensive behaviour, he was 'transferred to a private laughing academy in Westchester and given insulin shock–treatments. No deep attempt was made to diagnose my "case"—except . . . that I had hallucinated. . . . Factually, this was not true. . . . Like all the other patients, I was considered beyond reasoning with and was treated like a child: not brutally, but efficiently, firmly and patronizingly. . . . Private sanatoriums and state institutions, I realized, were isolation chambers rather than hospitals'. After release, and a relapse in which the temptation to suicide was successfully *resisted*, Krim too trustingly sought psychiatric help, whereupon, though 'very much in my right . . . mind, but too paralyzed by drugs to move, I was at once taken . . . helpless to protest . . .' to another hospital where 'electric shock clubbed my good brain into needless unconsciousness . . .Apart from . . . the unimaginative grind of occupational therapy, each patient was left completely on his or her bewildered own, a farcical sight when one considered the $125 per week that their frightened families were paying.

'I saw that nine-tenths of the people I was quartered with were not "insane" by any of the standards a normally intelligent person would use; the majority had lost confidence in their own ability to survive in the world outside, or their families were afraid of them and had palmed them off on "experts", but positively no serious attempt was being made to equip them to become free and independent adults

Still: Anouk Aimée and Jean-Pierre Mocky in La Tête contre les Murs.

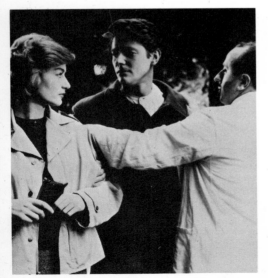

. . . they were palliated with pills or jolted with shock, their often honest rage echoed back to them as a sign of their illness . . .

It may be that what Mocky and Franju are saying about 'institutionalization' might have been more persuasively said in the more intimate, dramatic terms suggested by the analyses of interpersonal relationships developed by R. D. Laing and his co-workers. Indeed, the translation of such analyses into intimate, dramatic terms is a very natural step, taken by David Mercer, whose affecting TV play, 'In Two Minds', was, I believe, based on a case in Dr Laing's files, and put the case against alienists' inhumanity all the more effectively. From that point of view, this film possibly falls between two stools. On one level, its borrowings from sensational or romantic iconography (leather-jackets, the all-understanding girl) subtly discredit its accusations, while on another level, an overt, Cayatte-style battering of audience pre- and mis-conceptions would have been more consistent and effective. But when all this is suggested, and conceded, isn't it evident that, flawed as it is, the movie hauntingly paraphrases Krim's account of his experiences, and that Franju's points about the deceitfulness of the tulips, and the callowness of the gaily coloured bar, anticipate, in scenic terms, the criticisms which are increasingly being levelled against psychiatric practice?

Even the stiltedness in psychological development springs from Franju's humility, his reluctance to accept schematized non-intuitive knowledge: '. . . the psychology is inside the sufferer's head, it's something I don't understand, and I don't suppose the psychiatrists do either.' This seems to be largely true. True partly because of the disputes between psychiatric schools—the Eysenckians claiming that *nothing* goes on in the sufferer's head, except, presumably, random though repetitive associations which can be 'punished' out of existence.

True also because most of the little that is known about mental disturbance is known from the outside only, as it were—certain patterns are spotted, and classified, but their 'subjective correlative', the experience in consciousness, and still more on the unconscious levels, remains opaque. The suffering, it seems, is vastly greater than it appears to be—a patient recalled from many years' severe schizophrenia, during which he had seemed blandly unaware and unfeeling, recalled that he had noticed everything, and had been in anguish during every waking moment of those apparently vacant years.

Stylized in its evocation of madness the film may be; but what style! This is an aesthete's film in the sense, not of a self-regarding preciousness, but, quite the reverse, of a meticulous intensity in the use of the medium. If the visual intensity of the silent film had never existed, Franju would have invented it. Anouk walks towards the camera, turns at a right angle, peers curiously over a wall from behind which

75

drift the wails of a madwoman, turns and retraces her steps. The pattern has the finality of an Euclidean Q.E.D., its rigid reversal and angularity evokes helplessness, despair, a stiffening fear, a tightrope-walk over the abyss of madness-by-contagion. Like Murnau's and Lang's works, this is a protractor-and-metronome film, and the problem for the critic in describing such a style is that it no more translates into words than the languages of abstract art, or of kinetic art, or of the dance, to all of which it has some resemblance (being at once graphic-static, graphic-mobile and choreographic), but which it integrates, inextricably, into elements from the narrative arts—and narrative poetry at that. Poetry and geometry meet amidst these landscapes whose greyness is as charged and nuanced as the sky before thunder. In shot after shot, the white walls of the asylum enclose windows and open doors, or other apertures, through which black-branched trees and skies seem, not just a glimpse of freedom, but themselves subjected to the enclosing architecture, as sadly captive as pictures hanging on the wall. Sounds whose source we tardily or never see have the ominousness of perpetual dread, while Maurice Jarre's liltingly dissonant music recharges the desperate images with a half-ironic, half-demented gaiety.

Like Anouk's little right-angled march, the constantly enfolding walls comprise a variation on the film's visual motif: *la ronde*. Patients are exercised by trudging dully in a circle. Others are lured into venturing out of their solitude by standing in a circle and holding hands, a child-like gesture which they perform with a limp immovability, as if their souls were slaughtered oxen. Gérane, on his motor-bicycle, moves through a bumpy, lowering landscape, in swoops and whirls of movement. A water-sprinkler slowly revolves, like nothing so much as a weeping-machine. And, as Alan Lovell comments, 'As they make love, François undoes

Stéphanie's belt. Franju brings this to our notice by deliberately cutting back from the couple so that we see the gesture clearly. It seems to mean more than we see from the incident itself. The meaning comes, of course, from the fact that this is the first time in the film that formally a circle is broken. The sense of release in the sequence only lasts for a short time.' When François is recaptured 'the searchlight circles the walls . . .'. And is the patient sadly mis-potting billiards in the asylum playroom any madder than the patrons of the gambling casino, blinking with obsessive greed at the wobbling curve of a little white ball flung out from a roulette wheel? Is even the violent prisoner, who goes for a fellow inmate with a saw, more dangerous to society than Gérane senior, who brilliantly pleads in a court of law for a case which he knows to be unjustified? Is he any more dangerous than Doctors Valmont and Emery, who between them are set to leave Gérane in for the equivalent of death—life?

The close-ups of the needle sliding into the skin are far from being a cheap attempt to shock the spectator by stressing something which we all know hardly hurts at all physically. The needle is that of utter indignity, of being not simply silenced, but overpowered at the most intimate level of consciousness.

The actors are so exactly attuned to the film's atmosphere that, as Godard said, 'Maybe Franju doesn't know how to direct actors. But Mocky, Anouk, Meurisse, Brasseur have never been better, never has their direction been more *right*. They don't *act*. They *quiver*.'

In the astonishing glacial tension which Franju confers on Paris by night, as seen through Gérane's eyes; in the sad dance of young Lesbians in a club; in the curious complicity of non-contact between François and Stéphanie, as, each carapaced in black leather, they straddle his motor-bike, he clinging to it, she to him, the film establishes a prevalence of 'sane' loneliness which is almost as terrifying as the concentration camp quality of the institution. Indeed, mental homes are an early form of concentration camp, dating back to the eighteenth century. Before then the mentally unbalanced usually wandered freely, because people weren't very frightened of them. But, like the concentration camps which the British set up during the Boer War, the provision for the inmates was so derisory that asylums and concentration camps alike became mythic places of dread.

The callousness isn't particularly the staff's.

They merely execute society's ordinance that those who can't move to its accelerating rhythms and in its narrow grooves must be kept apart. The stray, the very young, the very old, the mad, are all out of step with the increasingly precise intermeshing of all our processes, are all too much for emotional arteries so hardened that they can barely stand the very minor strains of readjusting to people from other social classes, let alone to those who

Still: Anouk Aimée and Jean-Pierre Mocky in La Tête contre les Murs.

behave oddly or irrationally. Perhaps we take it for granted that institutions are the natural place for the mad, because even the peacefully, amiably mad arouse in us that excess of fear, that expectation of violence, which comes from our superego's brutality against our own peaceful but repressed irrationality, i.e., the spirituality whose permitted forms—mysticism, eroticism, and art—are all either etiolated or subversive. The problem is less the madness of the mad than the madness which they release in the sane. As Franju remarked, 'The manifestation of public opinion in the film is the hunter's shot, by which the absconding inmate is killed.'

'I respect nothing,' Franju observed, immediately adding, 'I respect the mentally ill, because I'm very close to them; and as they frighten me, I made a film which frightened myself, and everybody else as well.' But the fear, being that of an *admitted* complicity, is different from the transposition into psychic melodrama which fear undergoes when, being repressed, it is withheld from the reality-sense. *La Tête contre les Murs* attains the quality of poetic fantasy which makes it a minor classic; and it belongs to the crop of recent films on mysterious incarnations: Welles's *The Trial*, Resnais' *L'Année Dernière à Marienbad*, and Buñuel's *The Exterminating Angel*, which all take on an interesting new light if considered as representing the subjective delusions of mental patients.

Perhaps, on the analogy of a truly prophetic scenario, *The Cabinet of Dr Caligari*, for 'the asylum', we should read 'the system'. Only the other day, a doctor was not only arrested, but unnecessarily manhandled by two detectives and a policeman, for standing near the statue of Eros and blowing bubbles. Though causing no obstruction or annoyance, he was rather oddly 'bound over' by a lenient magistrate. No doubt he will be punished should he again perpetrate an eccentricity calculated to disturb the peace of a free country.

Les Yeux sans Visage

By his reckless driving, a brilliant plastic surgeon, Dr Genessier (Pierre Brasseur), is responsible for disfiguring his daughter Christiane (Edith Scob). Unaccustomed to being 'contradicted' by fate, he resolves to confer a new face on his daughter. His devoted assistant Louise (Alida Valli) drives into Paris, and lures students who resemble Christiane to Genessier's home; there he attempts, vainly, to graft their faces on to hers. At last his own face is torn off by the dogs on which he intended to perform experiments, and his daughter, still faceless, wanders off into the night. The doves which, for Franju, suggest madness, hover round her head, as if their fluttering were her shattered, freed thoughts.

'When I shot *Les Yeux sans Visage* I was told: "No sacrilege because of the Spanish market, no nudes because of the Italian market, no blood because of the French market and no martyrised animals because of the English market." And I was supposed to be making a horror film!'

For all these handicaps, Franju seems to have succeeded only too well. The French have always admired the English penchant for horror stories, and imagined that the land of Mary Shelley, Bram Stoker, Jack the Ripper and Terence Fisher would appreciate an artistically-made horror film. Alas, when it was presented in the Film Festival at Edinburgh (home of body-snatchers), seven people fainted, and public and press were outraged. Franju didn't improve matters by saying that now he knew why Scotsmen wore skirts.

In England, *Les Yeux sans Visage* was greeted with a unanimously shocked, or contemptuous, press. Critics were already disturbed by the Hammer horrors; and here was a horror film which really hurt. Almost the only reviewer in a national daily to give it a good review very nearly lost her job as a result—it's very dangerous not to conform in the world of English culture. The critics disagreed as to whether it was actually too horrible to bear, or whether it incompetently failed to horrify, or whether it incompetently failed in every respect except horrifying. (Needless to say, *Sight and Sound* bayed its utter scorn). However, the film's reputation was rapidly redeemed, partly by the younger critics (notably Ian Cameron), partly by the slowly percolating influence of the French magazines, and partly by the retrospective prestige of Franju's more obviously respectable films, including *La Tête contre les Murs*, which wasn't imported until after *Les Yeux sans Visage*.

That the storyline contains unoriginal ingredients can't be denied; here is the mad surgeon, the secret operating-theatre, the hounds. But a storyline, in itself, is hardly more significant than the storyline of a painting. In itself, it is a shell, which can be filled with rotten meat, or with pearls beyond price. The disparity between story and film can be suggested by indicating some stages which often

Stills: Les Yeux sans Visage. *Above—Valli and victim. Below—Valli, Pierre Brasseur and Juliette Mayniel.*

79

intervene. After establishment of the storyline (or scenario) comes the masterscene script (the film divided into scene-settings and written out as a play), the shooting script or *découpage* (the shot-by-shot storyboard), revisions suggested by the director (if he didn't intervene earlier) to suit his style, and then the actual filming, which is a synthesis of contributions by script, director, actors, and other artists, including the most unreliably brilliant of them all, chance. A director can utterly transform a film by his control over the last two stages, and if, as in Franju's case, he also controls the *découpage*, many a trite story can be completely exsanguinated and filled with new blood. At this stage in the rapid evolution of film criticism, it can't be repeated too often that visual content in a film is just as important as visual content in a painting. Literary content corresponds to the general outlines of a painting's composition, that is, to the cartoon. Some of the meaning lies here, but rather more lies in that network of significant details which we immediately recognize as a painter's style, i.e. vision, i.e. meaning, i.e. content.

This doesn't mean that there is any need to apologize for, or explain away the horror content of *Les Yeux sans Visage*. The horror genre is as much a part of modern mythology as the Western or the detective story. It's ironical that our mythology springs either from religion or from pulp pops. The mad scientist, like the gunslinger, is a figure in our pulp pantheon. As valuable an analysis of our society's stresses and strains could and no doubt will be written in terms of these contemporary archetypes as in terms of high culture artworks. In his sensitive acceptance of the *infra dig*, Franju is heir to Apollinaire, to Cocteau and Breton, who had spotted the poetry of Arizona Bill, of Mack Sennett and Fantomas two world wars before Anglo-Saxon *littérateurs* had even begun worrying about pop culture, let alone attempting to understand it. Franju hasn't the least

intention of diluting the story's pulp shocks, nor even of sublimating them. Poetic, like religious, myth, has every right to concern itself with the pounding of blood and the rumbling of thunder, with indelicate sensations indelicately rendered; its finesse lies in the grafting on such libidinous roots of the more delicate stems of feeling.

Thus the cliché aspects of the story can be transformed into poetry by the styles which bathe and impregnate them. In the opening sequence, the branches along a country road are spectrally illumined by car headlights, and seem to perform an eerie dance, emphasised by Maurice Jarre's waltz, as slippery as black ice. We are launched into a fantasy realm which is only the dark lining of our routine world. Photography becomes a medium in the spiritualist sense—this world speaks to us from beyond the grave, the grave of our belief that the everyday isn't eerie. The delicate loop described by a Citroën DS as it parks, the reflection of black branches in its black metal skin, the rhythm with which scalpels are placed firmly in Genessier's rubber-carapaced hand, the morgue by a Métro station near which the trains emerge like grey ramrods into listless day, cease to be 'superficial' details of style, they link the mythic and the everyday.

The film's physical details are as carefully orchestrated. One scene contrasts Valli's furs with Juliette Mayniel's raincoat; later Edith Scob in her white satin housecoat contrasts with Mayniel's rough garb of white towelling. The cables of an electro-encephalogram recall the surgical clips framing a face during an operation. The dogs wear studded collars which evoke slavery, while Valli wears a velvet choker, because she is Genessier's dog. Valli in a leather coat drags a dead girl, nude in a man's mackintosh, across rough ground in such a posture that it is almost a perverse embrace: Lesbian, necrophiliac, sadistic. Valli strokes

Still: Les Yeux sans Visage. *Patterns and textures.*

Edith Scob's hair with a reverent sensuality, and we are reminded of the Lesbians dancing together in *La Tête cóntre les Murs*. But Franju is not interested in the Lesbianism of Lesbians, not even the loneliness of Lesbians, so much as in a sad and sexless dislocation of being, a contact which is at once turgid and void. The loop described by Genessier's DS, seen from above, parallels the course of his pencil over a doomed girl's face, itself a disturbing parallel to the scalpel's subsequent curve along the same line.

Christiane, believed dead, lives in her snow-coloured apartment, like a soul in purgatory, amongst satins and glossy fashion magazines, with a transistor radio, and all the mirrors replaced with black panels. Flayed alive beneath her pearly mask, she murmurs through its unmoving lips into the telephone, her fiancé's name, and he hears her speaking as if double-long-distance from a satiny grave. Marienbad was a luxurious concentration camp of the soul. Christiane's secret rooms have the same resonance, and, like X and Y, she almost returns to

81

the land of the living. Overlaid sounds are used to 'enlarge' the screen—crickets whirring, the sloppy thud of a body into a family vault, the tired throb of a passing airliner. The movement of an automobile along a road takes on the quality of a strophe—Genessier's sleek black mirror of a DS glides soft as a shark, Louise trundles about in a 2CV, humble, rustic, like a barge, in fact, *le chaland qui passe* . . . .

Such details occupy the bulk of screen time, and might have weakened rather than set off the terror. Several factors ensure that they don't. First, the Boileau-Narcejac script is unconventionally, but effectively constructed. In form it anticipates *Psycho:* a first heroine visits 'Hell', is killed, and a second victim nearly takes her place. If the fates of these victims provide the principal melodramatic shocks, they also, as in Hitchcock's film, allow a certain dramatic and moral complexity. When Mayniel, having been facially skinned, escapes in Genessier's house, unaware, because of the towelling round her head, and drugged as she is, of what has happened to her, we hope she will succeed because where there's escape there's hope, if only of revenge. But we hope even more desperately that she will not escape, because then she will have to face the truth. And so we're caught in a tangle of hope and counter-hope, our optimism and pessimism are equally frightening, the melodrama loses all will-she-won't-she naivety and becomes elegiac. And when the girl lies dead, her eyes stare at us, unseeing, though slits in the towelling; hers are the eyes without a face, and, now, the eyes without the eyes.

But our principal, and subtlest, identification is with neither of these outsiders, but with Christiane, on whose behalf they are to be sacrificed. Through her, we find ourselves involved in a paradoxical concern for Louise, who loves Christiane and whose love Christiane appreciates, and even for Genessier, who at least plays a concerned paternal role. Maybe

his paternalism is an aspect of his megalomania, just as Louise's canine devotion is an aspect of her selfishness, a feeling that since Genessier saved her he can do no wrong. Provoked as quietly as they are, with direct confrontation reserved for the end of the film, the conflicts take on tones of regret, of puzzled guilt, of misplaced and doomed decency, which become the film's dramatic key, and impregnate the most melodramatic moments with deeper tones.

Second, Franju's style itself constitutes a unity, linking the everyday, the atrocious, the pessimistic, the demented, the beautiful. It's no

Stills: Les Yeux sans Visage. *Edith Scob at bay against the treachery of tenderness and domesticity.*

accident that our first identification, with a victim of physical violence, leads to an identification with a victim of mystification, whose one violent act springs from a reflex of compassion. Hence, though the film horrifies, Franju was right to resist its classification as a horror film. 'It's an anguish film. It's a quieter mood than horror, something more subjacent, more internal, more penetrating. It's horror in homeopathic doses.'

Inevitably, of course, critics who are hypochondriac about violence, or too coarse for poetry, or both, will respond only to the violence, which, torn out of its context, will seem either ineffective, or only too effective, depending on the pattern of their tabus and responses. But even more disturbing than critical reactions is the urban American response described by Pauline Kael in her stimulatingly demystificatory 'I Lost It at the Movies':

'The theater, which holds 2646, was so crowded I had trouble finding a seat. Even dubbed, *Eyes without a Face* . . . is austere and elegant . . . It's a symbolist attack on science and the ethics of medicine, and though I thought this attack as simple-minded in its way as the usual young poet's denunciation of war or commerce, it is in some peculiar way a classic of horror . . . even though I thought its intellectual pretentions silly, I couldn't shake off the exquisite, dread images.

'But the audience seemed to be reacting to a different movie. They were so noisy the dialogue was inaudible; they talked until the screen gave promise of bloody ghastliness. Then the chatter subsided to rise again in noisy approval of the gory scenes. When a girl in the film seemed about to be mutilated, a young man behind me jumped up and down and shouted encouragement. "Somebody's going to get it", he sang out gleefully. The audience, which was, I'd judge, predominantly between 15 and 25, and at least a third feminine, was . . . pleased and excited by the most revolting and obsessive images. . . . But nobody seemed to care what the movie was about or be interested in the logic of the plot.'

The psychopathic reaction has something in common with the critical one—both are blind to anything but violence. Fortunately neither is typical of audiences elsewhere. The present writer saw the film three times in upper working-class family halls, where the audiences were gripped from the opening moment by the intensity of atmosphere, and went on to a consistent identification with each victim in turn—sickened screams being provoked as Genessier lifts, from the bloodied front of Mayniel's head, the soft plane of her expressionless, eyeless face: and later, as his pencil marks out the next victim's face, the audience flinched as if the pencil-point were already a scalpel. If attention relaxed during one or two scenes, like Genessier's slow walk upstairs, which remain caviare for the general, the one detail of Franju's which, on the level of brutal efficacy, overreaches itself is

Louise's croaking 'Why . . .?' after Christiane has driven the scalpel into her throat. No doubt it's physically possible, since a scalpel is a delicate instrument, no doubt the reminder of anatomical intricacy is more disturbing than the usual 'bang you're dead!' stylization which renders movie violence so abstract; but the very contradiction of stabbed throat and speech is a little too startling for people to take, and needs a more analytical presentation.

One wonders, though, if Franju is really protesting against science, or medical ethics, *per se*, whether Genessier hasn't been too completely assimilated to Baron Frankenstein. After all, his motive isn't scientific curiosity, and his conduct is hardly ethical.

Still, the overtones remain, and are reinforced by the lecture of which we catch a glimpse as the film begins: 'the subject is completely exsanguinated', says the lecturer, whereupon the audience, including a Jesuit, bursts into applause. It's significant, too, that the graft Genessier attempts is currently on the border of science fact and science fiction. Plastic surgeons still have to take the new skin from another part of the patient's body, because, except in the case of identical twins, 'foreign' skin mobilises the home antibodies which attack it. Franju explained: 'The hostile antibodies could be destroyed by X-ray bombardment, except that the dose needed is so massive that it would kill the patient as well. The Yugoslavs have developed a bonemarrow graft, but the face is something else again.' Is it possible that we might one day soon have facebanks as well as bloodbanks and eyebanks, or even standardised faces which the body and mind would slowly remould and reinterpret? Genessier's innovations belong to the order of disturbing scientific possibilities, like immortality by deep freeze, and so do carry a Frankensteinian overtone, of sorts.

Obviously, though, Franju isn't indicting scientific hubris in the face of any divine or natural order. It is Genessier's will to power which brought about the road accident, which so distorts his love of his daughter, and which reduces other girls to abstractions. However pure and benevolent science may be, there is certainly a scientific callousness just as there is a militaristic, a moralistic, an ideological, or any other sort of callousness. We don't need to argue a case from recondite theories about surgery only being sublimated sadism to begin with. We've all known of doctors, midwives or nurses, who don't bother with anaesthetics even though the patient is screaming, or who, in various subtle ways, use the doctor-patient situation to gratify their sadism; we have all been treated as things by doctors, who look at our disease as if we weren't there. Again, it's an open secret that many of the regulations concerning the vivisection of animals are, even in the land of the R.S.P.C.A., honoured more in the breach than in the observance. Indeed there's an eerie echo of Franju themes in a recent anti-vivisectionist advertisement, showing a photograph of a dog on to whose neck a second (dying?) head had been grafted. The photograph, revolting enough in itself, especially since the second head is from a dog of a totally different breed, becomes even more upsetting if, following Franju's practice of identifying with the victim, one asks oneself: how bewildered is the second head?

One's impression that Franju's quarry is not science *per se*, but a certain use of science, is reinforced by the other aspect of Genessier's crimes. A clue is afforded by Louise's all-but-posthumous '*Pourquoi . . .?*' to Christiane, implying: 'I helped you, why stab me?' She can't understand, because she can't understand humanity, only loyalty. Genessier's callousness derives from a similar attachment, a sort of vicarious egoism, which, ineradicable in human nature anyway, derives a special resonance from the film's French context. For in a country whose bourgeoisie isn't so far removed from the peasantry, with its close, secretive family spirit, the cult of the family has a political connotation which it doesn't possess in England. The cult was a prop of Pétainist politics (as against the Resistance), and has long figured in all right-

Still: Les Yeux sans Visage. *Edith Scob wanders off-limits to find her father's next sacrifice.*

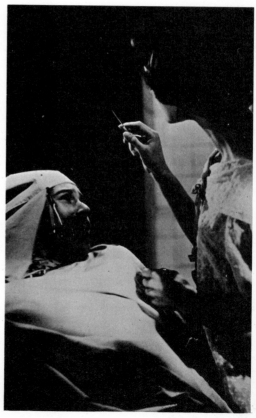

wing programmes for Moral Rebirth; it links strong puritanical overtones with conservative politics, being opposed to the collectivist ideology of the left. Ravaged by Genessier's familial egoism, Christiane can oppose to it, finally, only her sense of obligation to utter strangers, a sense of indiscriminate solidarity which here becomes a left-wing attitude. Franju doesn't show us Christiane's faceless face at the end, but I believe that as she walks into the night air, freeing the dogs and the doves from her father's cages, the ghostly face hovering over her scarred tissue is the most beautiful face in the world. She is mad, but her madness is an absolute, an impossible assent to freedom, to tenderness and powerless mercy. As the mad were thought to be, she has become divine.

In this affinity of angels and animals, of those above and below the routines of rationalist calculation, the film evokes a kind of moral metaphysic and acquires a theological ring. Dr Genessier ('Genesis') is God, who insisted on 'ruling the road'—Christian orthodoxy sees pride vis-à-vis God as the original sin, but an anti-Christian metaphysic might well ascribe the megalomania to God. His daughter, Christiane ('Christian') is his creature—a female Adam, a virginal Eve. But as Genessier doesn't rule the road, she has to suffer to redeem his pride, so she's also a female Christ (orthodoxy describes Christ as the second Adam). Louise is Genessier's Holy Christ, a dark angel selecting sacrifices. And in this black, inverted theology, it's not the Son of God who is crucified for man, but woman who is flayed alive to atone for God's mad pride.

These interpretations aren't offered in the belief that allegorising makes a film seem profounder than it is; it doesn't. But a profound meaning is held, as it were, in suspension by the intensity with which Franju's style extends a melodramatic idea into a mythological malaise.

86

Pleins Feux sur l'Assassin

Though dons affect the 'intellectual' detective story and deprecate the horror story, the two genres have the profoundest affinities. Historically, both descend from the Gothick romance, which in turn is an early Romantic adaptation from a folk tale form, the ghost story. In the typical ghost story, the wronged or vengeful ghost returns from beyond the tomb, and either hounds the murderer to his doom, or hounds someone else, like Hamlet, until he hounds the murderer to his doom. In the detective story, the corpse stays buried. And his avenger is a detective, working on behalf of society, rather than of a supernatural order, and in the rational terms of clues and deduction rather than irrational ones. In the most popular horror stories, the monster, whether wronged or vengeful, corresponds to the ghost, and sometimes he hounds his creator (Frankenstein) rather than his slayer. Inevitably, the innumerable permutations and variations deserve a study to themselves, but the pattern of sin-crime, death and revenge links the genres, which constantly shade into and combine with one another.

Thus if, on the one hand, the mystery story tends towards the realistic drama (like Simenon), on the other it relates to the mythic, and Thomas Narcejac admirably defends the possibility of intensifying its mythic resonance:

'Far from being a purely cerebral diversion . . . [the detective story] unleashes the nocturnal and animal forces of our imagination, educates or refines them, enables them to feel all the ambiguous aspects of a world which we wrongly believe to be purified of all magic, restores to us the sense of a universe which logical explanation is powerless to exhaust and from which the strange has yet utterly to be expunged. The solution doesn't mean a thing to the aware reader; what matters is the anguish; it's that

Still: Pierre Brasseur prepares to die in Pleins Feux sur l'Assassin.

keen sense of an unformulable peril which gives existence its weight, its density and its value . . . The detective story is a tale capable of becoming delirious to the exact degree which reason calculates.'

In what is (wrongly) called the traditional detective-story, the emphasis on detailed logical deduction can be seen as a rationalist defence against irrational (mythic) anxieties. A typical detective story might have the relatives of the deceased gathering for a reading of the will, and then being murdered one by one; in the archaic form of the same story, the heirs are being murdered by the ghost of the dead man. It's the archaic undercurrent which makes detective stories return to the theme of murder with a quite unrealistic obsessiveness. Where there's a murder, there's always a ghost, even if he's disguised as a corpse, and there's always an exorcist, even if he's disguised as a detective.

The work of the Boileau-Narcejac team is unequal, and if from a literary point of view it suffers from its very workaday prose, their best scenarios (*Vertigo, Les Yeux sans Visage*, perhaps *Les Diaboliques*) expertly cherish the interaction of rational and irrational anxieties. The storyline of *Pleins Feux sur l'Assassin* is all the more fascinating in that a strict Agatha Christie intrigue is unwound 'in those confines where dream and reality merge. One step further, and it's the other world, that of Odilon Redon and of Marianne Andreau. One step back, and it's only the dear old classic detective mystery, with its locked room, its red herrings, its suspects and its eccentric but brilliant sleuth. We are straddling an invisible frontier, like Charlie Chaplin in the last shot of *The Pilgrim*.'

These ambiguities bring Boileau and Narcejac very near Franju, the Surrealist realist, and even if they're very far from being the poets in prose that he is in images, it's no surprise to learn from them that 'He was an old friend even before we collaborated; we very much

admired his short films, Franju had read our books. For *La Première Nuit* he asked us to write a word of introduction, thinking people might otherwise be confused by it. . . .'

The Agatha Christie format is ingeniously and humorously inverted. All the rich relatives are hoping to inherit the family castle and its treasures from their malicious uncle, the Comte de Kéraudon (Pierre Brasseur). To spite them, he contrives to have his own corpse hidden, and tensions rise among the assembled relatives, for the law won't assume he's dead until he's missing five years, and while waiting, they're responsible for the upkeep of the castle. They arrange *Son et Lumière* performances to raise funds. But one of their number dies in circumstances suggesting foul play; another attacks a relative whom he finds with his wife; and as a *Son et Lumière* spectacle invokes the ghosts of the past, a woman commits an expiatory suicide.

The subject offers obvious possibilities for a highly critical view of the 'best people' (as the heirs bicker and squabble), of the cult of stately homes, of the *Son et Lumière* medium (whose message is a throwback to that romantic, elitist view of history which even our elementary schools are abandoning), and of tradition generally (for the present behaviour of the heirs blows the gaff on the past). The script is further spiced with trenchant asides about profits in Algeria, and a priest who specializes in waterdivining and radiesthesia; while the castle with its sombre, all-enfolding presence, could become as baleful as a psychiatric hospital, and does indeed become, as several French critics noted, the real star of the film, while its historical trophies evoke the trophies of *Hôtel des Invalides*. The play of *Son et Lumière* on castle

Stills: Pleins Feux sur l'Assassin. *Left—rehearsals and misadventures. Right—Dany Saval and Jean-Louis Trintignant as the lovers.*

walls was surely tailor-made for Franju's sensitivity with lighting and architecture. Franju remarked: 'It's a ghost story without a ghost. What I shall enjoy is making emptiness live.'

Yet of all Franju's features this is probably the slightest. In the first place, the intrigue is so intricate and obtrusive, yet so self-contained, that its resemblances to the *Ten Little Niggers* formula survive all the minor variations worked within it by its ingenious authors—it's a murder story without a corpse, and with only a peripheral murder. There were three possibilities of escape from the gravitational pull of the Agatha Christie spirit. First, as the critic Francis Lacassin, later Franju's scriptwriter for *Judex*, suggested: 'Never has a title been worse chosen than *Pleins Feux sur l'Assassin*. For all its only too commercial appeal, it has the major drawback of destroying the suspense from the very beginning. Without this wretched title, we would hardly have believed that the heirs who disappear one after the other could have been struck down by a merely human hand. With the mediaeval legend to reinforce the suggestion, one would have been able to believe in a series of fated coincidences, ordered and inspired by the Castle, outraged by the profanities to which it is being subjected. And the presence of an old owl, spiritual guardian of the stones, is most propitious to . . . the spell of a Radcliffian ambience.' One may suspect that such a theme might have needed more than a mere change of title, indeed, substantial revisions of the storyline, emphasizing the castle's physical qualities as a collective mantrap, or as a whale's belly, its gastric juices dissolving the minds of those lured into it by greed. Other possibilities include either an inspired way with the characterisation (one can imagine a Renoir revamping of the script, an appetisingly gruesome *La Règle du Jeu*) or an intensively Surrealist elaboration of a bizarrely elegiac atmosphere, so that the storyline be-

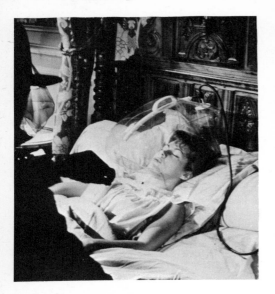

comes merely the thread of a series of dream-like episodes.

But Franju and his producers, it seems, were at constant cross-purposes, and, as he commented scathingly, 'You can't build anything on an avalanche of concessions.' One of the scenes he envisaged showed a strange young heiress riding through the forest with another girl on her horse behind her; the producer objected on the grounds that 'the public doesn't like Lesbians'. A sophisticated, but highly selective, sensitivity to sexual overtones *only*, is the most insidious form of censorship. It's ironical how the tabus on all expressions, and even sensations, of friendship between people of the same sex, are strongest, now, among just those people who are 'sophisticatedly' aware of sex, even when they claim to be broadminded in sexual matters.

A sense of atmosphere can only transcend such a story if it can find roots in the story ('it's

at the typewriter that you have to be inspired'); but if *Pleins Feux sur l'Assassin*, considered as a whole, belongs in the class of the 'quality thriller', it has the poetic cachet of its style and its scenes include several anthology pieces, notably the *Son et Lumière* sequence, with sound and light creating romantic hallucinations of the past, on which a present tragedy squalidly irrupts, and the final, jocular scene, where the curse of the past is lifted from its young lovers, as a massive black hearse rumbles on its way to the cemetery while overlaid, Georges Brassens meditatively strums, *Où sont les funérailles d'antan?*

Franju regrets the void left in the film by the absence of Edith Scob, whose tremulous radiance, even behind her mask, gave such beauty to *Les Yeux sans Visage*. The characterisation ranges from the characteristic detective story stereotypes to cameos which crackle with humour or tension, like Jean Babilée's amiable cynic, Marianne Koch as the Amazon equestrienne from the family's German branch, or the virile groom who, after a stable love-scene of some purity, rejects her coarsely because he's as patriotic as he's puritanical, like his co-servant, Joseph the gamekeeper, in Buñuel's *Journal d'une Femme de Chambre*.

Thérèse Desqueyroux

Although at the Venice Festival, Emmanuele Riva was awarded the Volpi Cup for her interpretation of the title-role, and Franju's adaptation of Mauriac's celebrated novel was greeted with respectful enthusiasm by the press generally, it met with a mixed response in just those circles which had championed *Les Yeux sans Visage*. *Cahiers du Cinéma* and *Positif* both ran unfavourable notices, later followed by defences of the film. The initial reports make a case against the film which, whether or not one in the end agrees, throws an interesting light on it.

Jean Douchet's note is worth quoting in full, as a little gem of discreetly subtle ironies. *Thérèse Desqueyroux* is 'its author's best film. Constrained to respect Mauriac's novel, Franju finds in the discipline a stimulus of inspiration. His film is sheer Delannoy—or it would be, were Delannoy capable of doing justice to Delannoy. There are some very beautiful examples of quality photography, of acting directed with as velvety a smoothness as you could possibly wish for, and landscapes in harmony with the torments of the characters. A real *Symphonie Stills:* Pleins Feux sur l'Assassin: *modern medicine and a secular ghost; a traditional hearse.*

Pastorale. Of the great Catholic novelist whose work has an odour of impiety, Franju—one must, after all, stay faithful to the image one has forged for oneself—has kept only the impiety. The film is as anti-bourgeois, anti-religious and anti-society as possible. Only Thérèse the anarchist is loveable. One reproach, though. It was a mistake to modernize the novel. In the epoch of the DS and the 404, it's no longer true that such a situation could have developed in just this way. The novel is dated and shows its age. Rejuvenation has only underlined its wrinkles and its grimace.'

In other words, Franju's most inspired film has all the academic qualities (the comparison with Delannoy), is old school ('the landscapes are in harmony with the torments of the characters'), is predictable in its attitudes (anti-, anti-, anti-), naive in its means ('only . . . the anarchist is loveable'). So much for Franju, whose best film corresponds to all that's worst of Mauriac's novel!

Douchet's deviousness is possibly inspired by discretion in the face of fashion; Franju's fellow-travellers, on *Positif*, prefer valour. 'Franju is made of sterner stuff' (than Godard), 'but he too belongs more and more in the past. *Thérèse Desqueyroux* is a solid film, well played; its evocation of an oppressively narrow society is convincing, but laborious. Everything is of a piece, in this stiff, bloodless work, dedicated to framing the performance of Mlle Emmanuele Riva much as, over thirty years, films signed Edmund Goulding or Curtis Bernhardt gave their all for Bette Davis and Joan Crawford. Here we are back in tea-room literature, where Franju wastes his time effacing himself behind Mauriac, just as he would be wasting ours if he set about presenting Duhamel, Bordeaux, Lacratelle and others of their ilk in the service of Jeanne Moreau, Madeleine Robinson or Annie Girardot. There's something very saddening in Franju's career, and his steadily widening distance from all the hopes we placed in him, his self-burial in conventional productions, in five-finger exercises of style, and in Selected Classics . . .'

The film's ready acceptance otherwise was doubtless facilitated by its very fidelity to Mauriac's novel, which conferred upon it an obvious 'literary content' and diverse kinds of prestige. And for the English reader, Mauriac's literary qualities acquire an additional fascination from the quality of his Catholicism, with its rare blend of modern socio-psychological realism and a rather archaic sense of direct metaphysical intervention. Mauriac's Catholic puritanism preserves much of the puritanism so familiar to English readers, but fascinatingly reverses some of its terms: the sins of the flesh are abhorred, but rapidly forgiven, while the sin which looms largest is that moral pride which is a Protestant virtue. And Mauriac's criticisms of Catholic piety dourly prick the bubble of indulgence to Catholic 'wisdom' which T. S. Eliot and others imported into the English literary fashions. What stands between Mauriac and classic status is, perhaps, that he quietly enjoys and exploits rather than explores major contradictions between a docile piety and an insight into the feelings behind its rejection, contradictions whose evasion is botched over with his weird swings between subjective, objective and God's-eye-view descriptions of his characters.

Defending Franju against the charge of effacing himself behind a writer who, without lacking moral courage, has never quite dared question his beliefs, Marcel Oms suggests that if *Thérèse Desqueyroux* is Mauriac's best novel it's because Thérèse is the one character to have escaped from Mauriac, to have become utterly and profoundly herself, to have cut off all her roots in religion and to have laughed to scorn all his tentatives to save or damn her. He returns to her in two short stories and a second novel, and finally 'saves' her in a third, *La Fin de la Nuit*; but all these sequels have conspicuously failed to attach themselves to her 'real' story, which is a matter of situation. Flaubert said of Emma Bovary, '*Emma Bovary, c'est moi*'; Thérèse is, if not Mauriac, at least, so to speak, his Mr Hyde: intelligent, dissatisfied, unreconciled, slightly demonic.

Hence no doubt the novel's fascination for anti-clerical directors: before Franju, Louis Daquin and Claude Autant-Lara had had hopes of adapting it. Hence, also, Mauriac's readiness to collaborate on the script with a director whom he must have known, if only through their third collaborator, his son, Claude, film critic of *Le Figaro Littéraire*, to be as anticlerical and atheist as possible. He must have known, too, that his name would enhance Franju's ability to resist official Catholic influence. As Franju testifies: 'I guarantee that if Mauriac's novel had been an original scenario, it would never have been passed by the censor. Never! . . . the Catholic Central Office was displeased with *Thérèse* [whereas Mauriac was pleased with it] . . . simply because my film didn't conform to the outlook of that miserable organization . . . If it weren't for Mauriac they'd have given me a great deal of trouble, just as they did with *Judex*. . . . They're strange, those people, you know . . . when Thérèse is about to poison herself, she's saved by the death of Aunt Clara. For them, this death is a divine intervention, as in the novel, they argue. Well, all right, I'm not an expert on the topic, but I feel it rather bizarre that for the sake of Thérèse, who isn't much of a believer, he should kill off Aunt Clara, who is. Ah well—mysteries of the Communion of Saints.' What Mauriac thinks of the scene in the film (as distinct from its original in the novel) isn't recorded; presumably we are in the presence of divergent interpretations as between director and screen writer. Similarly Alain Resnais and Marguerite Duras see contradictory implications in the final scene ot *Hiroshima Mon Amour*.

So far as its form and action are concerned, the film follows the novel very closely, omitting minor scenes, adding very little, occasionally altering the order of the major scenes to give a more direct dramatic line. Both film and novel begin with Thérèse travelling back from the court where her husband's evidence has cleared her of attempting to poison him. She reviews her life and their marriage in a series of flash-backs, but her hopes of a reconciliation are dashed by her husband and his whole family vindictively consigning her to 'solitary' in her bedroom. Eventually, abashed by the results of their callousness, they pack her off to Paris.

From one angle, the novel could be an attempt to give a God's-eye-view, i.e. a complete and compassionate understanding, of the way in which a sensitive, intelligent, scarcely abnormal woman could come to commit one of those cold, secretive, domestic crimes so characteristic of isolated rural districts. Though Thérèse is guilty of spiritual pride, the novel becomes an indictment of the society whose rigidities and restrictions of feeling are equally guilty. In his preface, Mauriac, in a rather Franjuvian sentence, speaks of having seen Thérèse's many originals 'at the mercy of lawyers whose hearts were less hard than those of the over-dressed women on the public benches'. It is clear that, for all their differences, Franju and Mauriac have sufficient in common to create a profound artistic reality of which different interpretations can then be made.

Claude Beylie suggests that Mauriac failed to realize that the cinematically far more sophisticated Franju was pulling a series of fast ones, as to just what certain scenes would imply; Claude Mauriac, as a very story-minded film critic, might be ill-equipped to decipher Franju's real implications. But one may prefer to believe, if only because it makes a more interesting point, that artists aren't always as jealously exclusive about their meanings as is often assumed by their interpreters and that Mauriac, confident in Franju's artistic integrity, was no less interested in Franju's Thérèse than he expected Franju to be in his. Since Thérèse's own attitude is, after all, nearer Franju's than Mauriac's, it is quite possible that Mauriac positively appreciated the way the film restricts itself to Thérèse's subjective experience, and exists in a key of materialistic sensitivity so near Thérèse's own. Like a playwright who is pleased to create a character whom x different actors can play in x different ways, Mauriac may have been pleased that his Thérèse could also be Franju's Thérèse—particularly since his preface indicates that she is in any case a 'type', for several different women whom he

Still: Emmanuele Riva as Thérèse Desqueyroux.

93

Still: a cosy family scene from Thérèse Desquey-roux.

has known or glimpsed, and who all shared a common predicament.

At any rate, the film depends on none of the ambiguities which one might have anticipated from the writer-director of *Hôtel des Invalides* or of *Notre Dame, Cathédrale de Paris*. The film loses the novel's religious frame of reference on the level of the script, rather than of the images. The action omits all dramatic or visual correspondence to the spiritual reference-points in Mauriac's prose. The commentary (spoken by the novelist) might have made a natural Voice of God, but it tells us only of

another aspect of Thérèse's moods. A devout Catholic, acquainted with Mauriac's novel and not suspecting any subversion, might quite easily, by some persistence of vision, experience the film as if the novel's frame of reference were perpetuated in it, though probably as many spectators would sense a shift of opinion as to human possibilities.

This can be most clearly summarized through the film's way with two of the novel's minor characters, the only two for whom, as for Thérèse, 'the life of the mind means everything'. There is a dimly-glimpsed priest, whose sermons she briefly attends, and the young, proud Portuguese Jew, Jean Azevedo. The priest and the Jew are both 'insiders' in that their cultures offer them sources of spiritual sustenance which Thérèse cannot find in the suffocatingly materialistic rural bourgeoisie. They are also complementary characters: Azevedo, matching Thérèse's spiritual pride as he matches her family's social pride, is something of a 'wandering Jew', steering by a divine discontent which, theistic rather than Christian, may well enable him to find his true self through the amoral experiences on which he is set as he leaves for Paris. Thérèse, less mobile, more profoundly moulded by her society, is both weaker and more destructive, and only as the novel ends has she found her way from various false goals—marrying into property, worshipping her own interest in ideas, suicidally destroying those she loves—to a simple dependance on human feelings, which she also finds in Paris. 'Life alone was interesting, people of flesh and blood. "It is not the bricks and mortar that I love, nor even the lectures and museums, but the living human forest that fills the streets, the creatures torn by passions more violent than any storm. The moaning of the pines at Argelouse in the darkness of the night thrilled me only because it had an almost human sound." '

In the film, the priest, who represents an unrealized possibility, disappears. Azevedo refers to Chekhov instead of René Bazin's life of Père de Foucauld. His pride is focused entirely on the human plane, merely playing with Anne, whose heart he breaks. In this context, even the film's structure, faithfully tracing the book's, takes on another meaning. Mauriac's flashbacks had the quality of a baffled psychological stocktaking, as Thérèse struggled to explain herself to Bernard and to herself. The film's flashbacks lack this quality of a psychological search; in Franju's words, 'the flashbacks are linked by the voices of François Mauriac . . . and of Thérèse' (a nicely Pirandellian touch). 'I played on levels of time, which increasingly interest me in the cinema. For example, Thérèse in the car, leaving Bazas after the acquittal is Tense 1. She thinks of a past scene, that's Tense 2. She sees an album of old snapshots which she used to dream over when she was still a child—that's Tense 3, the past in the past. That album prompts another memory which becomes a Tense 4—a sort of future relative to Tense 3.' Because the cinema's norm is still to be less nimble with time than verbal forms, these time-layers take on a quietly deliberate quality, and the search for motives is forgotten in a re-living whose mood is elegiac rather than fatalistic. The effect is all the more marked since the story itself does not need flashbacks for the sake of dramatic movement. They become as gratuitous as those of Max Ophuls, as charged with a sense of time itself.

The intricacies of time, the negations of its flow, that we saw in *Le Grand Méliès* affect this film another way. Mauriac's novel, published in 1927, describes a regional bourgeoisie as yet undisturbed in its thought by TV, by radio, by the social mobility characteristic of the 'sixties, by the modern acceptance of hedonism (particularly among the young). In the 'sixties, can the incarceration of Thérèse by her family, and, particularly, her acquiescence in it, still derive from thoughtless assumptions, or does it need some subtler explanation? Could any such explanation avoid turning Bernard from a decent enough, if brutally thoughtless, representative of a way of life, into a 'case', and Thérèse into her own executioner rather than a prisoner-victim? Would a girl of her spirit really resort to slow poisoning rather than just leaving? Would Bernard's family be so ashamed of divorce? Would Thérèse have married Bernard in the first place?

On the other hand, the artistic world, cosmopolitan as it is, and particularly interested in the various New Frontiers of social and intellectual thought, habitually underestimates the massive conservatism even of suburbia, still more that of cultural backwaters, more stagnant in France than in England. Franju points out that the houses which figure as the Desqueyroux and the Larroux homes were furnished, in the mid-'sixties, exactly as they had been in the 'twenties, though Franju doesn't say which generation inhabited them. Marcel Oms suggests that if the Desqueyroux of 1927 no longer typify the society of 1967, they represent a reactionary, and influential, element in that society. Much in Franju's film is confirmed by Claude Chabrol's *Le Beau Serge* and Francois Villiers's *L'Eau Vive*. Even so, one or two significant oddities appear on the surface of Franju's film. Thérèse has a record-player, but no radio, let alone TV set. She is driven home from the court in a car; but she and Bernard do not have one of their own. Nor is her isolation merely a matter of communications. Its completeness outdoes even that of Bresson's country priest: Thérèse has only her records, and classical at that, whereas he at least hears the music and laughter from the young people at a village hop. But Thérèse is supposed somehow to be a semi-emancipated, forward, spirited girl.

Partially valid though it is, Oms's defence of the film is outflanked by the conspicuous absence of young people in the film. For Thérèse belongs to both groups, and it is along the lines of this conflict, between the most deeply rooted and the most mobile peer-groups in the community that the story of Thérèse in 1967 might paraphrase those of Thérèse 1927. If Thérèse's theological sin is pride, might she not, as a proud girl from a reactionary family, adopt towards her own generation a pose which cuts her off from them, and forces her back to an older way of life? If the Thérèse of 1927 is relatively passive to ambient assumptions about marrying Bernard because of his property, might she not, simply, choose an older way of life as a gesture, and, when trapped, find it an empty one? In preference to hating herself (which she might still do on a conscious level), she becomes obsessed by a hatred of Bernard on an unconscious level, whence the 'inexplicable' murder attempt. She might well become an accomplice in her own sequestration simply because she is too apathetic to complain, let alone escape, and too intoxicated by a suffering which seems to justify her hatred and pride. It is, after all, by such subtler mechanisms, encouraging self-betrayal, rather than by less complicated confrontations, that society today breaks down the nonconformist. And the phenomenon of cultural atavism is interesting, in a generation much less emancipated than it is presented to be by the media.

It's often assumed that psychological precision is the touchstone of a narrative, and on that basis remarks on Franju's psychological archaism must seem to be pointing towards a radical flaw. But the fact that the story's conversion into contemporary terms can so rapidly be indicated suggests that the flaw is a relatively minor matter. After all, we perform just such paraphrases when we relate a novel by Lawrence or Hardy to our contemporary issues and experiences. If only the cars, dresses and record-player were of 1920 vintage, the film would be altogether homogenous. The real reason for its apparent updating is probably that audiences seem to dislike period films which aren't in some way romantic, extravagant or picturesque about their period. Mauriac's novel is forty years old; by the time

Franju's film is forty years old (2003), posterity may have only the haziest notion of how 1963's cars differed from 1927's, and the film's anachronisms will have faded into the background, where they belong.

As in *La Tête contre les Murs*, Franju is less interested in a superficially correct psychological articulation than in a study of solitudes so radical that they don't even appear to articulate —not only between people, but within the person, who is cut off from himself as from others, and exists, self-enclosed and sad, in his unit of consciousness, as it were, one-dimensionally. The discontinuous quality of flashback narration enhances the effect. Franju's disinterest in psychological explanation can become a deliberate 'obstructionism', of the highest type, that is, a preference for riddles and

Still: a proud proprietor. Philippe Noiret as Thérèse's husband in Thérèse Desqueyroux.

challenges. He describes Thérèse as 'a Bovary who strikes back' but 'after the last shot, she will still be an enigma, a challenge, still mistress of her own experience.'

Is this indifference, however deliberate, a flaw? Franju's 'I don't give a damn for psychology' may remind one of an interesting if debatable aside by Stephen Gottlieb, made with Buñuel in mind: 'I can now be specific about why paranoid artists don't interest me much. They have remarkably little interest in other people. In retrospect his characters are so unmultidimensional, so shadowy, that I am inclined to characterize them as the shadow figures of a paranoid consciousness.' Is, *mutatis mutandis*, something like this true of Franju, who so carefully subdues his actors to his own tonal and scenic schemes, whose vision is, in a sense, monolithic, from beginning to end, in depending on the direct interaction of his eye and the landscape?

Among the distinctions between Franju's Thérèse and the Thérèse of a 'Delannoy capable of doing justice to Delannoy', is that Delannoy would articulate everything with psychological and dramatic correctness, but without any shafts of surprising insight. However, Franju's is a world of invisible prison-cells, of solitary confinement in space, in silence, in the moment, a confinement imbued by lyrical intensity with the massiveness of fate, or of a virtual fate. Because Franju's temperament isn't one to waste its time on appearances, the possibilities of dramatic evolution are minimized. Moreover, 'correct' psychologizing would only distract from the sense of a profounder oppression. His films go straight to the underlying essential, and in this respect, again, the film's affinities are with Bresson rather than any conceivable Delannoy (a category among which Mauriac might be included). The sense of solitude in *Thérèse* is as oppressive as the physical violence in *Les Yeux sans Visage*; it

97

is indeed only another aspect of it, more insidious, because less conspicuous.

Franju's direction of the actors seems so velvety smooth because, wherever possible, he elides moments of dramatic conflicts, or confrontations, or softens and subdues them until they become almost 'scenic', that is, the juxtaposition of separate sensibilities. These may observe or palpate one another, and perhaps decide to absorb something from the other, more by a quiet recognition of unsuspected affinity, by response to invisible vibrations, than by the thrust-and-parry quality more conventionally attributed to human relationships. The flashback structure also enables Franju to cut when he wishes from the immediate action to a close-up of Thérèse, meditating, with an obsessive, more diffuse anxiety. And a strangely satisfying tension derives from the interaction of Franju's 'scenic units' and the script, which, considered in itself, has everything needed for smooth articulations.

Accenting the mood of the moment, Franju obscures the sense of dramatic movement, but in reality, many of our spiritual battles are felt more as drifts, of whose climaxes we are hardly aware. Yesterday, we were *there*; today, we are *here*. And so far as our own responses are concerned, that's all we know; all the rest is deduction, hypothesis and theory. It's not surprising that in this age of psychological theories (often very good ones) art has rapidly lost interest in psychological analysis, or relies on the audience to fill in such connections for itself. Indeed, the specialised public is *so* analytical that it enjoys wrestling with cues which are riddles of apparent inarticulacy—Campbell's soupcans. Franju's rendition of Thérèse as an enigma is reconciled with the appearances of reality, the emotional textures of his lyricism. Here as in other ways, he interrelates an avant-garde undertow with a sense of life as lived, which lacks certain aesthetic extremisms which are less avant-garde than cul-de-sac.

Usually, if a film artist puts himself at a distance from the subjective or immediate aspect of a scene, it is for the sake of emphasing an otherwise unobtrusive aspect which is nonetheless relevant to the narrative direction. In the simplest case, the camera lingers with unexpected pointedness on an object, whose significance is still unclear. Sometimes, though, this distance seems a function of something almost outside the narrative. The new emphases lead the mind to a 'vanishing point' existing behind and lacking in the narrative. So with Bresson's *Pickpocket* and *Au Hasard Balthasar*, whose reserve creates, as it were, spiritual space, in which God would exist if he were allowed into the characters' minds. In his overtly religious films, a similar reverse soft-pedals both the obvious religious factors, and purely human meaning, substituting the more metaphysical sensitivity which is Bresson's touchstone. Mauriac's story offers itself as a candidate for the same overtones, and one shot comes very near Bresson: a close-up of Thérèse's hand, as, deprived of cigarettes, she makes the obsessive gesture of smoking. The detail is in the book, but not the choice of close-up for it, as is clear if one imagines how Renoir might have rendered the detail—possibly with a roomful of people! But in Franju Thérèse's solitude remains too earthy, too pained. Each moment is a subjective space-time cell of its own, enigmatic and claustrophobic, something one undergoes as one undergoes pain.

The script refrains from gratifying much curiosity as to motives. Notably, it gives no indication whatsoever of why Thérèse thinks she wants to marry Bernard, or wouldn't mind marrying Bernard, or what the advantages and disadvantages would be. From a conventional point of view, this is a startling omission. The writing team of Jean Aurenche and Pierre Bost,

98

who worked for Delannoy and more important directors, and who, though a particular target for the pubertal rage of the young Truffaut, remain masters of the cinema's mainstream idiom, would carefully have included a scene introducing Thérèse's various motives for the marriage, and establishing their irrelevance to something in her spirit. But Franju simply states, and shows, her ravaged uncertainty during the ceremony. Journalists who can't stop laughing at the idea of the cinema being treated as seriously as any other art will no doubt fall right off their stools with hilarity at

Still: the wedding scene from Thérèse Desquey-roux.

the suggestion that if a film omits any of the psychological content of a novel, it could be for any reason other than the director's blunder-ing oafishness. Fortunately, the presence of the Mauriacs as Franju's collaborators on the script makes a good *prima facie* case for what Franju's own critical background and stature should make quite obvious: that the study of motiva-tion is quite deliberately abandoned. Apart from the artistic gains adumbrated above, the

99

covert parallelism between Franju and Robbe-Grillet returns to mind. Claude Mauriac, as a literary-minded film critic, and author of a good critical study of *L'Alittérature Contemporaine* as well as of one or two *nouveaux romans*, may well have been influential in balancing the script so finely between its traditional form and the avant-garde undertow.

For Mauriac, Thérèse's quest for contact is an aspect of her quest for God, but the theme of Franju's film might be summed up by the question: 'What do the characters want from one another, and from the world?' Their own confusions about this are a main cause of their suffering. Fascinated by Anne, Thérèse is easily rebuffed by her innocent indifference, and later so convulsed by jealousy of her happiness in love that she sets out to destroy it, and becomes, as Anne accuses her, 'just like them!' In her parting scene with Bernard, she realizes why she wanted to kill him: to see a flicker of uncertainty—of real *response*—disturb his complacent composure. She imagines the pines speak to her of freedom, which she fails to recognize as only an echo of human passions.

In a film about loneliness, it is appropriate that relationships with people should be evoked in terms of relationships with objects (pines for people). Thérèse has to be warned against starting a forest fire with a dropped and carelessly extinguished cigarette; her nonchalant destructiveness is prefigured as, later, she 'carelessly' begins to poison Bernard. His proprietorial concern for his pines parallels his concern for Thérèse, who exists only as wife and container for his heir. And Bernard's abrupt shift from panic, when he thinks it's his forest on fire, to bovine unconcern, when he discover it's only his neighbours', gives Thérèse

Stills: Thérèse Desqueyroux. *Hunters and victims: Thérèse, Azevedo, Anne.*

the opportunity, and idea, of poisoning him in an equally unconcerned way. The last shot, of the Paris streets in which Thérèse loses herself, insists that she is very likely to be as lonely here as among the pines; visually, we are extremely conscious of variations on the forest motif: a line of spiked railing, with ranks of pollarded trees beyond; the people seem lost among the stone. In *Thomas l'Imposteur*, too, there is a conspicuous example of a key scene's visual contradicting the commentary on it.

The pines motif is counterpointed by the cigarette—one remembers the link of cigarette and factory chimneys in *Théâtre National Populaire*. How delicately Riva catches the awkwardly fashionable gesture with which she holds her cigarette, not so long ago a symbol of feminine emancipation and fast living! In the country she is drastically careless; during her immurement, her cigarettes are taken from her in case she burns the sheets, and her empty fingers perform the gesture, as of a ghostly identity. Free in Paris at last, she grinds a cigarette end under her heel, and Bernard drily comments: 'Afraid of starting a fire?' Here, too, she is an ill-adapted creature caught between two worlds. The transition from the danger of burning a forest to the burning of sheets is a substitution of a type familiar in poetry and dream. There is a similar transposition between the birds, which Anne kills, and Thérèse's child, whom Anne looks after. The cigarette motif, and Anne's relationship with the birds are not invented, as an *auteur* theory might suggest, by Franju, but feature prominently in the novel. The riddle posed by Anne's delight in wanton slaughter is resolved, not too obviously, by the 'anticlerical' comment, also from the novel: 'The nuns of the Sacred Heart had interposed many veils between their pupil and reality.' The riddle's solution, like all good solutions, introduces a new, subtler dimension of atrocity: how total and abject is the blindness of

this de-natured angel! Art, after all, is as much a matter of goading a spectator with good riddles as of explaining things to him.

The scene crystallises, in extreme form, the theme of psychological communion (which, in Mauriac's work, ultimately relates to communion with God), of 'innocent cruelty'. Bernard isn't intentionally cruel to Thérèse; he's not lacking in natural curiosity, but coarsens it into thoughtless possessiveness: he's taken aback when his wife doesn't want to show him Anne's private letter to her. Even in his imperceptiveness he has a kind of vulnerability. Through his hypochondria the little boy lost inside him clamours for tenderness which he doesn't know how to give or ask for. In a Freud-saturated age it's reasonable to see his hypochondria also as a self-punishment for the sexual suffering he inflicts on Thérèse. Even his brutality towards Anne is a matter of panic, of feeling out of his depth and therefore clinging to patriarchal rules, which sweep everything aside in an automatic obedience to the 'right thing'. This contrasts with the conscious malice of which the more lucid and independent Thérèse is quite capable.

Occasionally one may feel that Riva maintains too much grace and passivity, even in malice. Yet this too is a radical paradox of her character. Before meeting Bernard again, when she lies deteriorated in solitude, she gazes at her haggard mirror-image, smiles, and decides to tidy herself up. 'After all, I mustn't frighten the poor boy too much. . . .' Few lines illustrate more clearly than this, with its hints of superiority, docility, masochism and irony, the complexities that can arise from the interaction of one terse line of screen dialogue and its context. The art of screen dialogue is nearer even than playwriting to the terseness of aphorism and apothegm. The line exists in the novel; but whereas the film easily and naturally isolates phrases in a visual context, the novelist needs a verbal continuity, and tends to reiterate the basic issues in so many forms and words that he never realises how few words he could use if he could give each phrase its full value. This is particularly difficult for the English, who are all cowed by Shakespeare's prolixity; the French, with the economy and balance of their classical tradition, are vastly better screenwriters. Cocteau's novels are extremely aphoristic in style.

By the end of the film, Thérèse has changed, Anne has changed, even Bernard has come to the possibility of change: his assurance vacillates, he says, '*Naturellement, uh, sans doute, enfin, il me semble . . .*', which is a nicely progressive gradation. And Thérèse has realised that she wanted to get through to him, which she hardly tried to do, or only by the grand perversity of attempted murder. They could almost start again together, though it's important that they can't.

The old servant who becomes Thérèse's jailer has the same locked-in quality. (An early shot, showing a similar old woman ringing a bell to call the girls in for a meal is overlaid with a commentary mentioning that she's deaf.) In her turn, she is a victim: Bernard, having, in his rage, left ambiguous instructions as to how Thérèse was to be treated, now threatens her with disgrace and dismissal for having treated her as she, with her older generation's rigid censoriousness, thinks he must have meant. Here too, Franju finds in Mauriac an ally in his criticisms of the reactionary concept of the family. Thérèse enrages Bernard by remarking that only the servants tell the truth about the family's past. Glancing through the family snapshot album, she sees certain conspicuously empty spaces in its white pages, from which the portraits of numerous black sheep have been removed. The family isn't at all the kindly, loyal community which the word suggests. On the contrary, it *obliterates* those who menace

its self-esteem, just as Bernard, fearing scandal, seeks to obliterate Thérèse within the house: she might be among the attendants of *La Tête contre les Murs*. Now that alienation has become a vogue word, it's worth remembering that it has its traditional forms, that there is a form of highly principled rigidity which dehumanises as ruthlessly as anomie (Durkheim's term for the chaotic lack of a moral hierarchy). The looming loneliness in the city hints at anomie, as Franju, calmly pessimistic, considers all the possibilities of things going wrong.

Half-separated from the action, the characters carry a particular, an existential weight, a sense, distinct from their solitude, of the profound privacy of being, which, though lyrical and stylistic rather than analytical and explicit, can justly be compared to the existential view of man as, not a solitary being who contracts into society, but of man as a social animal who constantly misses integrity as he fudges all sorts of confused compromises between society and solitude. Bresson relates his characters to God *or* nothingness, rather than to the more conventional polarity of good and evil, whose corollaries Mauriac unpredictably concedes or denies. Franju relates his to their own fulfilment (in poetry) or to a grimly painful drabness, often unconscious of itself, but leaving its trace in tired, cowed or mean faces. The dimensionality of Franju's characterisation comes less from articulation and evolution, though all the principal characters in *Thérèse* evolve, than from degrees of reserve, relative to the moment and the face. In a sense, it suggests depth through an absence of depth (by showing *only* a façade, he gave houses mystery). His is a negative rhetoric, like Bresson's. In both directors, acting begins, not with a glance directed at someone, but with the glance directed at no-one (as in the quiet, ingrained rage of Thérèse's father, which focuses on her only because it is there within him, constantly).

102

Still: Riva as Thérèse Desqueyroux.

This eloquence, purged of display, this quality which Godard calls 'palpitating', gives richness, mystery and a quality as of frailty to every gesture, every pose, every mask. In the case of *Thérèse* there is thus no need to explore the social context in itself—sawmills and so on—because the social context is interiorized in the principal characters themselves, and acting which goes deep enough, which relates to private being, must constitute a social analysis which may or may not be related to outward terms. After all, that of *Thérèse* needs very little explanation.

Every shot bears the stamp of a virtuosity that has long dispensed with rhetoric. Two girls in white cycle through the fields, but their apparent freedom is belied by certain immobile details. A stone house-front catches the sun, the silhouetted serrations of agricultural machinery mark out the space around them. A field at night becomes a circle of torchlight shakily questing and flowing over dark tree-trunks and telegraph poles; the countryside, too, is a menacing chaos. Franju's combination of long shots and long takes permits so deft a dovetailing of movements within the frame and camera movements that the film possesses both a steady movement and an oppressive claustrophobia; in this respect, it is a minor *tour-de-force* in the Murnau idiom. As Thérèse resolves to destroy Anne's happiness, she tears up her letter and throws the pieces from her hotel balcony; they flutter around her like the birdwings of madness, a panicky fragmentation of the mind.

Jarre's music is dominated by the piano, which, for Franju, symbolises the life of the provincial bourgeoisie. Like many of Franju's apparently private symbols, the association is truly poetic, being condensed rather than arbitrary. The piano is the instrument par excellence of the romantic yearnings of the middle-classes. It is the instrument of the home, of the individual playing to a small private group. It is a piece of furniture, a piece of valuable property. Through it, the individual commands something of the resources of the small orchestra—for the same reason, it is the instrument of loneliness. At times Jarre's score seems to me too sumptuous in its compassion to take the edge off pain, notably when Thérèse is sequestrated and disintegrating. The contrast is quite deliberate, though. Nor is Franju too concerned that Riva, at a key moment, is far from being as haggardly ugly as she should be to justify the start of horror by Bernard. This stylisation is quite common in the cinema, for obvious reasons; you can't starve your actors, and though the cinema may be a visual medium, this in no way commits it to being a realistic one. We can all accept the reaction shot as being the true indication of what we haven't actually seen in her.

In its steady pace, its monotonal visuals and mood, its frugality of gesture, its terse and enigmatic characterisation, and its longshots, the film quietly splits us from the rise and fall of the turmoil in Thérèse's breast. This fits the fact that, throughout the first half, Thérèse is remembering, endeavouring to see herself and others objectively and dispassionately. In the second half, when the film is no longer in flashback, Franju deepens the involvement—there is even a first-person panning shot round Thérèse's prison. But here too the film sometimes combines Thérèse's self-involvement with Franju's detachment.

At a first viewing, the film occasionally irritates as Franju quits the faces, which are interesting us, in which we look for nuance and development, for the landscapes which echo their moods as dissatisfyingly as the pines. At a second viewing, we realise that this is intrinsic to Franju's sense of solitude; we, like Thérèse, are forever baffled by faces and can find release only in the pines or the sky. It relates to the curious dichotomy between visual and commentary. From one angle, this paraphrases Mauriac's own curious switches between 1st, 3rd, and even 2nd, person narration, one such switch occuring even in our brief quotation from the book's last page. From another angle, it establishes the element of mystery, of ellipse, from which springs Thérèse's seemingly whimsical consent to her own crime. Her mood is in the pines; her mind is merely lucid. She exists partly out there, and partly in here, but in a torn-apart, spreadeagled way, a schizophrenic 'bilocation' which most of us have experienced, even if only in the banal form of 'The sky is happy, why aren't I?' Here 'the sky is gloomy, it presses in on me, but I am so steely-cold.' This critic still wishes that, at one point, Thérèse had become herself, had become *ugly* with malice, with frustration.

One finds similar lacunae not only in Bresson, but also in Dreyer's *Ordet* and *Gertrud*, subjects not so far removed from *Thérèse*, the first as a study of a spiritually dead rural bourgeoisie, the latter as a study of an emancipated woman. Franju, like Dreyer and Bresson, has restricted himself to an emotional key-signature to which the full range of obvious reality is then edited to allow the spectator no respite from the unremitting pressure of a character's fundamental, and essentially passive, confusion and pain.

An unexpectedly discontinuous movement, a slightly too sumptuous music, a refusal of psychologising, a subtle detachment of subjective and objective, a meditative distance in time, an excessively graceful reserve in Riva's playing, a sophisticated stylisation; the interaction of these qualities and flaws perhaps accounts for the impression of academicism which the film leaves after a first viewing, but which begins to dissipate with a second, until, at a third, it is revealed as an almost unbearable cry of pain.

It's ironical that, in this 'interior' drama, Franju's way with dark landscapes should faintly recall Anthony Mann's *The Furies* and *The Tin Star*; a certain stoicism may be the subjective correlative behind both their styles. More profound is the recurrent Franju-Resnais affinity. As in *Hiroshima Mon Amour*, Riva is both repudiated and sequestered by her family; Resnais, also, tells us all we need to know about her father in one brief shot of his immobile face. Stylistically, there is a telling contrast with a film which, it seems, was originally written by Jean Genet for Franju to direct: Jeanne Moreau as *Mademoiselle*, another dissatisfied intellectual, deliberately sets fire to the forests surrounding her loneliness. It is intriguing to make a mental comparison between Tony Richardson's mighty barnstorming and the restrained tensions Franju would have brought to the subject.

Judex

'I wanted to make *Fantomas* and they offered me *Judex*. I seized the opportunity.' Louis Feuillade directed the first version of *Fantomas* in 1914. A serial totalling eight hours' screentime, it centres on the exploits of a popular pulp villain, whose crimes, as huge and more ingenious than those of Dr No, mesmerised the movie public, delighted the Surrealists, and mobilised the self-appointed guardians of the nation's morality. Feuillade enraged them again with *Les Vampires* (1915), but *Judex* (1917) and *La Nouvelle Mission de Judex* (1918) arose from his desire to create a good *Fantomas* and so square the tastes of the masses with middle-class morality.

Franju's version is based on the first *Judex* serial. According to this, the dishonest banker Favraux made odious advances to Judex's mother, and, when she scornfully rejected him, ruined her husband, who was driven to suicide. She made Judex swear to wreak revenge. A master of disguise, he becomes Favraux's right-hand man, the apparently aged Vallière, then, when the time is ripe, kidnaps him. Favraux has a widowed daughter, Jacqueline; when her daughter's governess, the dark and sullen Diane Monti, gets wind of Judex's schemes, she rescues Favraux and kidnaps Jacqueline. But

Judex enjoys the aid of a comic private detective, Cocantin, and of an urchin called Le Mome Réglisse (The Liquorice Kid). The battle of wits concludes with the triumph of good over evil.

Though less demonic than its forerunners, *Judex* retains something of their magic, born of that strange osmosis between the dream-like and the realistic engineered, perhaps not altogether unconsciously, by that 'honest artisan', Louis Feuillade, who was also the second founder, after Zecca, of movie realism. (Truffaut's reference to the Lumière Brothers as founders of movie realism has been too easily accepted, by this writer, among others: the Lumière Brothers made moving snapshots, and never understood the cinema. As Franju remarks, the antithesis of Méliès fantasy is Zecca realism.)

Breton and Aragon commented: 'It's in *Les Vampires* that one must seek the great realities of the century. Beyond fashion. Beyond taste.' The great reality evoked in these Feuillade serials is a psychic one. Just as sexual repression with its hysterias and melancholias ravaged the nineteenth century, so the psychic scourge of the twentieth is paranoia (with an apathy of emotion). Feuillade's serial epics of criminal persecution are poignantly balanced between the two moods. They first adumbrate the secret, shadowy power-structures which proliferate cancerously through Kafka, in '1984' and William Burroughs, and are currently reaching some sort of climax on the entertainment level in the current multiplication of thrillers involving mysterious world-dominating and world-protecting entities (UNCLE, SPECTRE, THRUSH and so on).

Entertainment tastes usually have some sort of parallel on the level of serious thought, and this vogue seems no exception. Throughout the century the bureaucratic network has tightened its grip on all our lives, and other networks of manipulators have become more prominent (if you detest advertising, opening a magazine or walking down the street can be persecutory experiences). So far as government is concerned, the masses refer to the shadowy and omnipotent Them, middle-class people gird themselves to resist 'faceless men', and even political scientists have to ask themselves 'Who has the power?' Society, too, seems adept at inculcating alienation, anomie, and all the other aspects of the individual's loss of unity and confidence vis-à-vis the group. Psychology has long concerned itself with the individual's tensions, but only now is it beginning to study relationships between individuals. The tensions created by all these uncertainties find an appropriate image in melodramas with a paranoid tinge.

This isn't to say that paranoia is a twentieth-century invention; only that it has evolved a new, prevalent form. We now are more conscious of the decisions made at our expense by society than of the threats posed to us by natural forces, and we are more sceptical about Gods and devils (earlier paranoid polarities). For us, Browning's phrase about catching 'the powers at play' is less likely to evoke visions of natural forces, or of a God or Gods, than of a committee shuffling through documents, or consulting its computers before deciding which would be the optimum moment to start World War III. Now we all live, as Kafka lived, under a bureaucratic régime whose absurdity has become apparent (and because it is apparent, there's a certain hope).

Up to a point, one can correlate paranoid art with the breakdown of social structures. Kafka lived under the shadow of the old Austro-Hungarian Empire's bureaucratic system. Feuillade's serials coincide with World War I: in the year of *Judex*, the French armies mutinied. The golden era of paranoid movies, the German silent cinema, coincides with the riots and inflation of the 'twenties, and, as Kracauer

shows, the persecuting tyrants who, from Caligari to Mabuse, crowd German movies, only predict their objective correlative, the Führer of the Third Reich. There are, of course, various other preconditions for the artistic flowering of paranoid forms. For example, there must be more responsiveness by art to reality than there was under Stalin, but not sufficient lucidity to permit the real causes to be clearly studied as problems in themselves. Today it's the spy fantasies, with girls galore and Technicolor to cheer us all up, which provide much popular entertainment pabulum.

Paranoia, in entertainment as in psychology, goes with megalomania, and the age of Kafka has also produced a special kind of super-hero, the clandestine crusader typified by Superman or Batman, who differ from romantic or folk heroes by the curious aridity and rigidity of their personal atmosphere. Judex and Batman are both formed by working back from per-

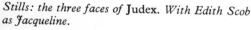
Stills: the three faces of Judex. *With Edith Scob as Jacqueline.*

secutory figures. Batman has many conventional devil characteristics—a black cloak, a horned hood, a batcave as H.Q.—while Judex, as we have seen, is a Good Fantomas.

Batman and Superman are simple and boring figures. But Feuillade was working in the shadows of the popular romanticism of Dumas, Hugo and Leroux, which was more warmly human than American culture. Feuillade himself was a director of realistic dramas. What is likely to surprise the 1967 spectator of Feuillade's *Judex* is not simply that a brooding atmosphere replaces the American obsession with speed, but that considerable time is devoted to the character's emotional reactions. *Judex* is to its best American equivalents (*Evils of Chinatown*, for example) as, say, Pagnol is to Sirk. Judex himself is deeply affected by his

mother's griefs, whereas Superman's parents are unearthly, and Lois Lane's indifference to the plain-clothes Batman isn't presented as a tragedy for him, as one can easily imagine it becoming in a French equivalent. Although the idea of a French version of *Batman* may raise a smile, it's worth pointing out that Judex is the original caped crusader, and that the first American serials of Pearl White were initiated by the New York branch of Pathé, still a French company, which was looking for subjects to compete with the immensely popular serials which Feuillade was directing for Gaumont. It's true that the American genre evolves out of the French and isn't just an imitation of it. But, historically it is really a dehumanised and, in a sense, degenerate development from it.

Feuillade's Judex is a curious, self-contradictory figure. Springing from a paranoid mood, he is himself a good negation of it. Thence problems. If he's ruthless, he's unbearably

107

priggish, and too cruel to be a hero, but unless he's a hero, he's merely a man. For these reasons, the Surrealists and Franju consider the serial an admirable second best to its predecessors. In its contradictions there can, though, be *mystery*. And the mystery in Franju's *Judex* has another dimension. Franju is an anarchist, a subversive who has been able to express himself in his chosen medium only by a veritable *tour-de-force* of tact, ambiguity and subterfuge. As an artist, Franju always has been, quite literally, persecuted by Them, just as Feuillade was. Franju, seizing the chance to remake *Judex*, was also concerned to subvert its moralising, to repudiate almost everything his hero stands for.

There are various possible ways of doing this. For example a brief phrase could give Judex a completely different set of motives. But Franju never takes the easiest way out by making alterations so extensive that the spiritual link with Feuillade is lost, and only the shell of a story unites them.

For an English spectator, the film's genre and tone are likely to introduce further confusions. Surrealist criticism, extremely influential in France, especially in film criticism, is virtually absent in England, where the 'poetry of pulp fiction' is correspondingly *infra dig*. The nearest equivalent to this interest is 'camp' but this, being essentially satirical, is its diametrical opposite. Second, Franju's film is a variation on a specimen of *naif* art, but itself exists at a rather different level of aesthetic sophistication —the *faux-naif*.

It certainly seemed to puzzle two English audiences at the Paris-Pullman. They accepted it from the beginning with a quiet interest, though also without great enthusiasm, as a refreshing oddity. Influenced, perhaps, by the film's sedate tone, they passed over its jokes in silence. About halfway through, though, taking their cue from the developing role of Cocantin

the daft detective and little Liquorice, they decided that the whole film must be a camp spoof of itself, and began to laugh, not only at the jokes, but at every improbability, even the very dream-like shot of four men climbing slowly up the side wall of a house. But to take the film on a camp level is as odd as it would be to take *Alice in Wonderland* on a camp level. Indeed, the difference between Franju's *Judex* and the audience's reading of it parallels the difference between Lewis Carroll's story and Disney's adaptation of it. The more delicate tones are lost, together with the logical structure and the balance of wonder and humour. For reasons of puritanism and class snobbery alike, English criticism in the 'good taste' tradition has no terms, still less antennae, with which to discriminate between the sensitive and the insensitive use of pulp imagery; still less between the *naif* and the *faux-naif*. After all, to make a camp cult out of Batman is pretty facile, since the serial was made twenty years ago and meant for ten-year-olds even then. The cult's real target is the moral simple-mindedness which American pop culture, more than English culture, scarcely outgrows. French films have never had to contend with anything like the same pressure of puritanical and omnipotent fantasies. If the tone of bitter-sweet disillusionment weren't deeply-rooted in French pop art, then 1940, Dien Bien Phu and the collapse of the Fourth Republic would have introduced it. There would be absolutely no point in spoofing *Judex*; on the contrary, the interesting thing would be once more to cast the magic spell, to make a Judex which would possess in 1967 not the suspense, but the poetic density of 1917. To do so, the film would have to be more than a reproduction of an antique; it would have to allow for the fifty years that intervene, and to use them somehow in the picture.

We have already indicated Franju's interest in nostalgia and time; *Judex* is the flowering of that nostalgia. It is set not only in a past tense, but in the negative subjunctive, the tense of 'If only things still happened like this, but they don't, and, alas! they never did. . . .' If that seems forced, how else can one define the film's action in relation to the shock of the final title, relating the film to '1914—an epoch which was not in the least happy'? And how else can one define a fairy-tale for adults, that is, for people who no longer believe in fairy-tales?

If the film is short of a masterpiece, it is a

Still: Judex—*the nightwalkers.*

little classic in a neglected genre in which we can place Feuillade's original, Korda's *The Thief of Baghdad*, Brabin and Vidor's *Mask of Fu Manchu*, Zugsmith's *Evils of Chinatown* and Roy Rowland's *The 5,000 Fingers of Dr T*. Whether their iconography derives from the fairy-tale, from pulp fantasy, or from science-fiction is of secondary importance. After all, Judex, with his hounds and his H.Q. in a ruined castle, is the last knight-errant, a chevalier whose black is the colour, not only of his menacing anonymity, but of his contempt and grief for the world's ways. He is something of a wizard, with his Art Nouveau closed circuit TV invention and his conjuring tricks, which cease to be tricks and become something more archaic: *marvels.* Like all wizards, he crosses the frontier separating the land of the living from that of the dead: he 'kills' Favraux, removes his body from the grave, and incarcerates him, underground once more, in a limbo which recalls *Huis Clos*, except that the damned man has for company only unseen watchers, and a mirror in which to watch himself deteriorate. Chance, too, dances to the tune of destiny. Judex presents Jacqueline with a cage of carrier-pigeons, with which to summon aid. When a villain, disguised as a plumber, enters the house, only to fall to his death from a ledge, a pigeon is accidentally liberated, and reaches Judex in time for him to rescue her from a *subsequent* murder attempt. When Judex himself is held captive in the deserted house by Diane and her minions, he is rescued by Daisy (Sylva Koscina), a circus acrobat whose caravans just happened to be passing that way. Preparing for action, she graciously removes her tiara, and her cloak, to reveal her fringed white tights. As in childish fantasy, she is always in her circus get-up—a charming detail which recalls Prévert's poetry, and, equally, anticipates the child's-eye-view of another lovely lady acrobat, the girl with whom grandfather

109

eloped in *Giulietta of the Spirits*.

Our first glance of Judex, at the masked ball, has a mythic force which can't be attributed merely to the imposing bird-masks which the dancers wear. Its secret resides also in the graceful sharpness of Judex's movements, as against the floating to-and-fro movements of the dancers, in a décor which contrives to be at once sumptuous and funereal. The description 'Surrealist' hardly catches the flavour of a scene which becomes the purest mythology, and, indeed, commences with a magical act. Judex, a black, fierce, lofty-crested mask rising from his chest, recalling also the plumed casque of a chevalier, pauses as he sees on the balcony a pigeon, his kith and kin, lying dead. The great bird-God takes the limp white body in his hand, gazes down at it in grief, though the fierce bright eyes and feathers show also a divine indignation. He holds the dead bird accusingly out to the guests, then gives a twist of his hand and the bird flutters away, alive and free. Thus, magically, he undoes the harm done by men. From the dancers, a cry of amazed pleasure goes up, as if, by this restoration, they felt absolved. But that assumption arises from their own folly: Judex has come to kill.

Thus presented, Judex, although he's also in evening dress, although the mask is only a mask, ceases to be a man. He becomes the incarnation of a demiurge, of a restorative and avenging force which comes from beyond morality, from nature itself. Like the totems of primitive tribes, he links the human, the animal and the divine; he is man as animal, and animal as God.

Gradually, he loses his divine stature and becomes merely a formidable man in a cloak, and finally a prisoner of the villains, indeed, a rather stupid fellow, for when the seductive governess declares her love for him, he turns

Photograph (above): Scob and Bergé. Still: Bergé and Koscina in Judex.

his head aside from her kiss with the puritanism of a Batman, instead of double-crossing her, as that bird-God would have done. In view of Franju's extremely sophisticated documentaries, there seems no reason to suppose that the hero's decline from the supernatural to the banal should be attributed to the director's insouciance, or incompetence; in any case, the progression is far too smooth, too invisible and dream-like for such interpretations to ring true. Strange switches from the superhuman to the vulnerable are, of course, common in myth. And if we allow that the logic of poetry may parallel that of the dream, then the pattern of Judex's moral diminution resembles the myth of the God who, descending among mortals, is humiliated and destroyed. The film's coda, a scene as tender as that of the masked ball is accusatory, completes the Frazerian cycle. Happy and secure, Judex and Jacqueline stroll by the seashore; tenderly, Judex turns and deftly, from gently cupped hands, produces a dove for her; she quivers with awe. It's still much more than a trick; it's both conjuring and conjuring up. It's the dove of poetry, the bird whose life is just a trick and yet—magic. As Matthew Arnold said, 'Poetry is spilled religion.' So are conjuring tricks—whose association with religion is a venerable one. A trick is supernatural for those who don't understand, and real poetry, as opposed to its academic counterfeit, is at once disbelieved and believed. This power is no longer the prerogative of a God, but that of a man seeking to please a woman, and, in so doing, frightening her a little, as all creativity is frightening. The God who came among mortals has been slain, and reborn as a man. A film which promises to be a paranoid epic concludes with this celebration of male tenderness.

Precisely the same diminuendo occurs in the film's science-fiction aspects. Judex begins as an electronic wizard, with all the gadgetry of Favraux's cell. Judex then offers Jacqueline the archaic protection of carrier pigeons. He is finally dependent on Cocantin hurrying off to use an ordinary telephone. The diminuendo is also in Feuillade, where Judex becomes ordinary as the drama takes over. In Franju's curter film, the drama is kept in its place, and Judex's irrational, but poetically right, descent takes on a purer line.

This is not, of course, to insist that such a pattern must have been (though it may have been) conscious in Franju's mind, any more than the pattern itself was conscious in the minds of those who created the myths in which Sir James Frazer discerns the pattern. But if the same theme, stripped of the dramatic complications in Feuillade, had been brought into the storyline (which is the textbook thing to do), then it would have come very near to banality, by its very resemblance to the modern, debased melodramatic equivalent, exemplifiable in terms of the Batman series. The whole point of Batman, as opposed to Superman, is that he has no super-powers: he can't even fly, he's simply human, and he can be briefly, potentially permanently, humiliated by, and this is significant, slick, jeering-type villains, the Joker and the Riddler. Catwoman completes the trio of American he-man fears: of slinky (i.e. homosexual) smart alecs, of intellectuals and of women. Batman is constantly on the verge of humiliation; he's the father/big brother whom the child (Robin) roots for. His defeat would hurt the child far more than his own. The theme runs through popular entertainment with an emotionality which conventional critical procedures never reveal but which showmen know all about—it inspires the consolatory epitaph over King Kong: 'The planes got him.' 'No. Beauty killed the beast.' In this sense, *Judex* is so similar to *Batman* that its reduction into terms of suspense would lose the mystery which it retains because Franju has left the theme where so much of poetry's meaning always lies: in atmosphere, in implication.

The film's mute tensions are intensified by a further point. As we've seen, *Judex*, like *Thérèse*, is a subversive adaptation. Judex, in intention, is a conformist hero, a super-cop. He can put right what the law can't, because he works outside the law. How far Batman and other super-heroes really represent America's latent Fascism is a matter of controversy. In the 'sixties, Feuillade's Judex, with his black cape and hood, really could evoke an important right-wing terrorist group of the 'thirties, the *Cagoulards*, with their extensive establishment network, or French Fascist programmes for moral reform, from which tycoons like Favraux were not to be spared. His kidnappings really could link up with abductions by the OAS or that para-police group the *Barbouzes*, while his concern with his mother's virtue is not only late Victorian, but makes him a pillar of, in the political sense, *la famille*. All this is quite conscious on Franju's part; he also remarks that the prose of Arthur Bernede (who scripted the 1917 *Judex*) is so cluttered with anti-Semitic asides as to be unreadable. Of course, we were all innocent in those days; no-one noticed that Sapper was as nasty as Ian Fleming and more dangerous, because less aware of it. It took something as explicit as *The Birth of a Nation* to arouse alarm. Anxiety about the ideology of thrillers remained at the rudimentary level of whether they made the novel, or the cinema, a school of crime. Indeed, however priggish the 1917 Judex may, by modern standards, be, Feuillade does his best to rescue him. He wants to forgive Favraux, and it's his mother who refuses to release him from his path, and treats him to a harrowing flashback of his father's death. Not only does Feuillade's film become almost tender towards the unhinged Favraux, but Cocantin, sitting by the shore, sheds a quiet tear over the villainess whose perfidious charm had also enthralled him, and us, in *Les Vampires*.

Franju, making a film for the relatively aware 'sixties (and for his infinitely aware *amis inconnus*) was concerned, so to speak, to deconformise it further, while retaining the general similarity necessary for his film to be nostalgic and wistfully ironic. First, Judex's motive is quietly changed. Judex 1917 is revenging parents ruined for a mother's virtue (a situation in a distinctly puritan tradition). Judex 1963 is concerned with compensating Favraux's victims with his ill-gotten gains. Judex 1917 might just have been a founder-member of the Paris branch of the Ku-Klux-Klan; the 1963 Judex is Robin Hood who has exchanged his Sherwood Forest green for urban-industrial black. Of Judex in 1917, one asks, 'Who? Why?'. Judex 1967 is a bird-God who needs no motives, because Franju's velvety style provokes acceptance as of a dream. Nothing impedes him from yielding to his scruples, and he kills, or attempts to kill, none of the villains, a function assigned to chance, i.e. destiny, i.e. poetic justice. Judex ceases to be a rather priggish and latently nasty Super-cop. He becomes the incarnation of a child's faith in, and the adult's nostalgia for, some mysterious being who will emerge from nowhere, and redress the wrongs of this mad world. He is an impossible character, like Giulietta's grandfather, who cries to the little girl, now a grown woman, as he leaves on his *Judex*-era aeroplane, 'Farewell, Giulietta, you have no more need of me, and anyway, I was entirely your own creation.'

To say that he is an impossible character, is to say that he is a psychic archetype within us all. Because that's what he is, he doesn't really need motives, and the motives Franju gives him (Robin Hood-ism) are an ethical, and political, orientation. All children, it seems, need to identify with a father-image who's pure and invincible, and even if we're lucky enough to outgrow it, that nexus remains in our minds.

It's a nexus which helps the right-wing to have ready access to people's imaginations, and which the left-wing finds hard to handle for a diversity of reasons. The element of arbitrary strength offends its preference for reason and justice. The father-image links closely with authority, tradition and prohibition, thus posing problems for reformist and revolutionary parties, which often prefer goddesses of liberty. The left's great venture into what Gordon Rattray Taylor calls 'patrism' (Stalinism) was a disaster. In a sense, Franju's Judex is that archetype related, experimentally, to a left-wing categorical imperative (if the rich have swindled the poor, you set about them on behalf of the poor). Judex comes from nowhere, because he is a secret agent from some parallel universe. He incarnates a moral attitude, and the film derives some of its mystery and its sadness from the tension between his despotic judge-jury-executioner role and his tenderness to victims, to Jacqueline, to pigeons. He shrinks in stature in this respect too; the film is about the acceptance of one's own fallibility, and the need to forgive. Judex forgives Favraux for the sake of Jacqueline, a procedure which is natural but is an offence against justice, and Judex thus resigns all pretentions to being a judge. He simply becomes a brave, decent, fallible man who has to be helped by Cocantin, by Réglisse, by Daisy, and doesn't mind at all. On this level, too, the film begins in a paranoid-megalomanic atmosphere, and then turns against it.

From another angle, the priggish, terrifying Judex is a symbol for the superego, not in the popular sense of the word, which is more or less synonymous with conscience, but in the more accurate sense, whereby the superego is a split-off part of the id, functioning as ruthlessly and unconsciously as the id. In a very real sense, children need to believe in an internal superman, usually based on daddy, as a defence against the supercriminals—the vampires—of their own paranoid fears, i.e. their fears of their own repressed hatreds of the parents. Judex and Batman, as we've seen, bear traces of their fearsome origins.

Judex, as superego, is 'corrupted', i.e. humanised, by Jacqueline, through whom he becomes capable of pitying and pardoning Favraux. His resurrection of the pigeon is supernatural, and his conjuring up of a dove from nothing is poetic—paralleling the shift from the unreality of the superego to the reality-awareness implicit in tenderness and reason. Judex is a superego which abdicates because love has taught it that it's too rigid and righteous, that if there's Favraux in Jacqueline there must, somewhere, be Jacqueline in Favraux, that it is itself wrong even when it's right. But, as an inevitable archetype, as part of the childish psyche living on in every healthy adult, it's also right even when it's wrong. Franju's tenderness and firmness raise and affectionately lay the ghost of the Manicheanism that haunts our minds. He creates characters who, in Claude Beylie's words, are 'waxworks of a baroque dream', yet endure contradictions and changes in the course of their phantasmal dance.

If Judex 'descends' (and ascends) from the bird-God to the human, the forces of evil, too, are reborn. Diane Monti is merely human in her motives (she wants Favraux's money), in her means (eavesdropping, burglary, disguises), in her weaknesses (for Morales, her rather limp gigolo-accomplice), in her treachery (turning from Morales to Judex, who is worthier of her mettle), in her courage and resourcefulness. The nearest she gets to divinity is in her disguise as a nun, a disguise whose overtones didn't fail to offend the Catholic Central Office, as we shall see. She, too, has a certain mystery. From the beginning of the film, Favraux wants to marry her, and she would only have to say Yes immediately to possess half his fortune, which she loses because she says No. Is it that she's too proud, too independent, to settle for half—she wants it all, whatever crimes that may involve? Is it a fairly obvious ploy by a gold-digger who's got her man in her pocket and wants to seem spiritually expensive too? If the latter, an element of mystery, of self-assurance, of very highly controlled cupidity, gives her as much stature as if it's the former, and her magnificence is only confirmed as she leads her lover and gang through one criminal exploit after another. Her overtures to the trussed-up Judex have an immediate appeal to the audience too: were Jacqueline even slightly less magic than Edith Scob, we would positively long for Judex and Diane to forget everything and everyone, to leave Favraux in his repentant condition, forget his fortune, and go off together, like Vincent Price and Linda Ho at the end of *Evils of Chinatown*. Franju delicately plays her slim, catsuited body off against her strength of will; another secret of her fascination is that 'Francine Bergé is an utterly frank person, and like all frank people, when she's in a bad mood, she looks terrifying.'

Human as she is, she, too, is worthy of a relationship with an animal divinity. An early shot opposes her to the bird-headed lions crouching in stone in the grounds of Favraux's mansion. Later, as she and Morales carry Jacqueline's chloroformed body away, they are confronted by the strangely silent hounds which appear out of the night, as if from nowhere, and watch menacingly until they have relinquished their victim and gone. Finally, as she lies dead among the cow-parsley, Cocantin's little friend Liquorice looks down at her with tears in his eyes. There follows a slow dissolve to the empty sea, and a second dissolve to an Alsatian couchant near the child whose governess she was. Reincarnation is too simple a concept, agreeably supported though it is by Agel's reference to Franju's Hinduism. Pan-

theism, perhaps, is a better word: the life-force which was Diane Monti has returned to the great formless pool (the sea), of which the Alsatian, as both guard-dog and wolf-dog, threatening and protective alike, is another crystallisation. Eisenstein often advised his students to correlate each of their characters with a particular animal, and does it himself, crudely, in *Strike*, and more sophisticatedly in aspects of *Ivan the Terrible*, where Ivan's robe trails like a snake, his bodyguard has an owl's round eye. If one applies that line of thought to Diane Monti, with her nocturnal habits, with her polite, stealthy egoism, with her status as a household 'pet' (governess), and with her velvety refusal to be owned by her master, then she's of the feline species. It's not at all an accident of language, for the idioms refer to feline characteristics, if she wears a catsuit, commits cat-burglary and meets her death on the tiles. Her tragedy is, in a sense, that she's too domesticated by the system to want to be as free as a bird, but she's too free to want to befriend man as a dog will.

What we have analysed in mythical terms can also be sketched, as Ian Cameron has done, in terms of time-structure. Art Nouveau, Cameron suggests, is associated with Judex and Jacqueline; it is an optimistic style for a period when the energies of the French nation seemed boundless. But by the outbreak of World War I, to which the film's last title refers, Art Nouveau was fifteen years old, so that it's already a nostalgic optimism. Thus Judex and Jacqueline represent the past. And Diane, scheming to win Favraux's fortune, not by assuming the bonds of old-style holy matrimony, but by a suffragette's 'equal rights' daring, represents the future. Hence, in Cameron's words, 'it's essential to the Brave Old World theme of the film that the figures representing the future should be the heavies'. But she comes before her time, the future isn't

114

yet ripe, and she falls and dies, in her way a martyr to the future, like Le Grand Méliès and Monsieur and Madame Curie.

Her reasoning is right, as far as it goes· 'Favraux earned his fortune by swindling everybody, haven't I as much right to it as he?' So she has. But his victims have more right to it than she. And she can't take the step that the otherwise more traditional Judex and Jacqueline have taken; of forgetting money, and substituting tenderness and concern. She's the future in some ways, but she's bound to the system's past in others, and she perishes at the hands of a man who represents not only the decencies of the past, but, in that rare, longed-for conjunction, the decencies of a possible future.

The affinity between Diane Monti and Modesty Blaise hardly needs stressing. So far,

Still: Francine Bergé in Judex.

it seems, the styles to which society is tending are represented in pop movies not by the heroes, who are almost always conservative figures, but by figures intermediate between heroes and villains—either sympathetic villains, like the early Bogart and Monroe, or villainous heroes, like Brando. Richard Smith has traced a similar evolution in screen décor. In drama, he says, modern furnishings were associated first with the gangster or ruthless tycoon, then with the sinister-friendly psychiatrist, and finally with the American hero. It's probably linked with the fact that screen villains are usually more realistic than the heroes, for obvious wish-fulfilment reasons. If you look at American movies up to the mid-'fifties, except for a brief interval during the disillusioned years before the Hayes Code was introduced in 1933, then the villains are almost the only males to strike modern spectators as not being pathologically deficient in their sexual aims.

Favraux is a characteristically subdued Franju villain. He indulges in financial chicanery, which is pretty normal for his time and class, and, in his dull panic, attempted murder. He hardly realises that he is wronging his daughter by the marriage which he arranges, in the interest of the family's financial connections, with a callow scion of the money-grubbing aristocracy. After his reincarnation by Judex, and the perfidious, but touching cares of Diane Monti, almost his last words are, 'All I want is to live unknown and in liberty.'

That Favraux is a symbol for a thoroughly corrupt capitalism is a point that shouldn't need stressing. His fortune is firmly fixed in historical fact: says old Vallière sadly to Jacqueline: '*La fortune de votre père se basait— comme, hélas! bien d'autres! sur le scandale de Panama,*' which, in 1892–3, exposed the widespread corruption linking French politics. This, and the 1914 war, are the two historical facts to which the film is anchored. Since we will no

115

doubt be accused of yet another mirth-provoking delirium of interpretation, it is pleasant to be able to reassure our more sympathetic readers that, far from being purely fortuitous asides, these two little details are all that remain from Franju's original intention of anchoring the film, firmly and with obvious critical purpose, in the realities of its time, by means of newsreel material and faked photographs showing Favraux hobnobbing with distinguished historical figures. The enterprise was abandoned because the rupture of style would have been excessive and because the film's running time was already longer than expected.

Again, our suggestion that Diane's disguise as a nun carries a hint of irrespect, not to say mockery, may seem absurd or far-fetched. But all poetic imagery is logically far-fetched. And not only did Paris-Pullman audiences gasp at Diane's masquerade, sensing the impiety, but the Catholic Central Office in France objected to the scene where Diana Monti, having to swim for it, strips off her nun's garments and stands, legs astride, over the camera in her catsuit—a scene carrying a further oddity: several French critics have referred to it as a strip, and that's the impact it has, though the stripper remains covered from neck to toe throughout. 'The Central Office wanted me to cut the scene in which the girl undresses. . . . Having shot it in one long take, I couldn't. And it's a pretty shot, and I refuse to cut into a pretty shot. And it's not scandalous, because everyone knows that she's not really a nun at all.' All the same, it *is* scandalous. If the Canadian and Spanish clergy had no objection to that scene, it may be because French Catholics, like French thought generally, have a special sensitivity to ideological implications in art. The Sisters of St Vincent de Paul, whose uniform Diane borrows—probably because it has the most birdlike headgear—didn't object to the masquerade, but they were shocked by the scene which showed Diane Monti's headdress actually touching the ground. They were also upset by a brief close-up of a cover of the original edition of a 'Fantomas' episode, which showed Fantomas and Inspector Juve, both disguised as nuns, shooting at each other across a coffin.

Jung, Robert Graves and the *Zeitgeist* generally have interested the intellectual public in the idea of Mother Goddesses and female animas, and father-images are out of fashion; the term patriarchal is almost synonymous with reactionary. Again, *Judex* has the quality of a throwback, being a celebration of father-figures. In Gordon Rattray Taylor's terms, it is patrist, like the nineteenth century, rather than matrist, like the twentieth. Judex, the young, invincible avenger, disguises himself as Favraux's aged, docile secretary, Vallière. Favraux, in his quiet way, has a patriarchal grip on Jacqueline: widowed though she is, and a mother, he is arranging her second marriage according to his own wishes. Kerjean, the old tramp whom Favraux runs down in his automobile, is about to be killed by Morales when a ring reveals him as his antagonist's long-lost father. Father-son relationships are reversed, in wish-fulfilment style, by Judex's protective or authoritative way with all the other characters, and again in the comic relief, provided by the interplay of a childish man (detective Cocantin) with a precociously knowing lad (Réglisse). The former spends the time when he should have been guarding Jacqueline for Favraux telling her daughter Alice stories from 'Alice in Wonderland', and he studies detection by reading 'Fantomas'. And quite right, too, for if he hadn't just been reading the bit where Fantomas and Juve both dress up as nuns, he might not have taken Réglisse seriously when the boy rushed in and blurted out his strange tale about Jacqueline having been kidnapped by a gang of doctors and nuns.

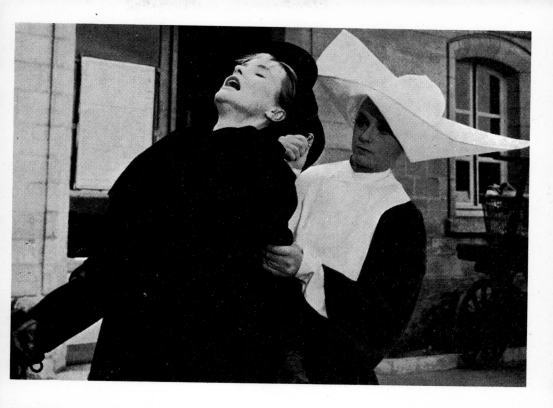

Still: Judex. *Francine Bergé and Edith Scob.*

Though it's subordinate to the patrist structure, there's a matrist pattern too. Diane, running Morales and her gang of toughs, is a young matriarch, and in that way too ahead of her time, anticipating Modesty. To the exhausted Favraux, she lies as to a child, yet soothing his male dignity. 'I'll watch—when I'm tired, you'll relieve me. Now, sleep . . .' It's so perfectly what a mother might say to a little boy who wants to prove what a big man he is, but applied to an old man, her employer

and husband-, and/or murderee-to-be, the pattern of contradictory levels is extremely disturbing. In no sense, though, is the battle between Judex and Diane a battle for authority between the sexes, in which female emancipation is associated with evil (a common puritan-influenced pattern). Diane is matched, finally, not by the patristic Judex, but by the providential Daisy. The old fairy-tale bogey of the wicked stepmother is paraphrased in Diane, the governess of the little Alice, who sets out to kidnap or kill Favraux, Jacqueline, Alice and Judex.

117

In critical discussion of archetypal patterns, it is often assumed that the mere presence of such symbolism in some way accounts for the effect of a story, imbues it with a cogency and resonance which stories without such patterns don't possess. Although the arguments would take us too far from Franju, one can at least suggest here another viewpoint: that any story effectively told will pick up the energy involved in these archetypes, that even political discussion can tap that energy, simply through the associations of words and concepts. The archetypes in *Judex* are no more classical than those of many thoroughly banal or boring movies. The archetypes do not redeem a banal melodrama; on the contrary, Franju's poetic style reactivates the archetypes and brings them alive once more. It may be objected that we have made the film seem profound only because we have analysed its basic structure, which all films, good or bad, possess, that if there's nothing other than a basic structure to analyse, it must be a pretty thin film. But what's interesting about *Judex* is that we become aware of these basic things in a truly poetic way. We don't penetrate to them at the end of a long analytical process which is inevitably quite separate from the experience of the film. On the contrary, it is a distinctive feature of the film that these basic patterns and simple details are brought poignantly alive by the miracle of style without intervening layers of rationalisation, without 'apparent' themes and false trails. Thus the film has its purity of nostalgia; it brings us to a never-never land, where these archaic things are no longer buried.

Franju asked his cameraman, Fradetal, for a style which was 'between earth and sky'. In Beylie's words, 'day and night, black and white, nun's headpiece and catsuit, thus perform a sumptuous "hesitation-waltz", an elegant *pas-de-deux* which confers on the work its indefinable and bewitching surface, as of a crepuscular choreography'. Just as in *Les Yeux sans Visage*, Genessier's Citroën reflected matt black branches on its shiny black surface, so here Diane's catsuit as she towers, legs astride, over the camera, reflects the silvery shimmering of the mill-race below.

An effect fumbled in *Le Grand Méliès* now enjoys a splendid flowering. Cocantin and

Still: (left): Judex. *Frame (below):* Le Grand Méliès—*shadows and frosted glass.*

Réglisse pass a bistrot, and the camera lingers on a blaze of lit frosted glass, a pattern of intricate corruscation, existing, strangely, on one flat plane. Then Cocantin opens the bistrot door, and through the narrow opening, a whole busy scene of animated customers drinking and merrymaking is revealed in depth. The play with space and depth is as sophisticated as anything in Dreyer. Apart from the contrast between a glittering stillness and warm crowded life, we are kept out, like Réglisse, from an adults' world, and we are kept out as moderns from the lost past. Life is hidden from us, weirdly, by a cold façade. All *Marienbad* is in that shot.

The effect is evoked again when, from the street below, Cocantin and Réglisse watch Diane, sumptuously gowned, open the brilliantly lit upper window of a derelict house, gaze out alertly, and close it once again. The house is of a type not unfamiliar in 1963; its tense is now. But a window opens, and there for a few seconds is the past in its full glory, and then it's gone. The situation wouldn't have the same effect if a child—two children?—weren't involved, for the separation also evokes the Oedipal sadnesses, envies, jealousies that loom so large in fairytales. In dream terms, or poetic terms, it paraphrases the situation of a child lying in his bedroom alone, and his mother, splendidly dressed, looking in to see if he's sleeping; he realises, perhaps for the first time in his life, that she's lovely, that he's alone, that she's lost to him. Yes, of course, here the mother is inside, the child is outside, mother is now an evil governess. But such reversals are also part of the language of dreams, which is why they require interpretation. Such a blend of strangeness and familiarity is exactly analogous to the barge being in a field instead of the water.

Another detail: when the carrier pigeon returns to Judex's hilltop castle, the camera-angle is so selected that the pigeon moves *upwards* on the screen to land, not, as conventionally, downwards. Nor is it a chance that Diane, dressed in her nun's habit, wears a crucifix swinging at her hip and directly beneath it has a glittering dagger strapped to her thigh. The spatial pun has an effect analogous to the flick-knife-in-the-crucifix in *Viridiana*.

The bird-masks beautifully lend themselves to Franju's sense of plane. Familiar as we are with the human face, it's relatively easy for us to deduce a profile from a full face, and vice versa (though we get surprises). But with these strange bird-masks, there seems some strange disjunction between profile and face; Judex or Jacqueline have only to turn their heads to create a change which is a visual and poetic event.

These remarks may seem forced, only because it is extremely difficult to describe subtle visual effects in words. Yet nothing we have said here is anywhere near as abstruse as many current interpretations of abstract paintings, or, for that matter, of music. In music, after all, the connection between physical detail and meaning becomes extremely abstruse, if you try and explain it in words. But it still makes us want to dance, or weep, or think profoundly, or all three, and there's no reason to assume that film directors are any less capable than composers of arranging subtle effects.

The film's principal weakness is the playing of the American conjurer Channing Pollock as Judex. When Franju accepted him, 'all I knew was that he looked like a fashion plate; and then I learned that he was a magician, so that he would have beautiful gestures'. No doubt Franju reckoned that, since Judex is a dream-figure, since he spends half his time disguised as Vallière, acting ability in the conventional sense is not a primary consideration, and that the atmosphere could say whatever the actor couldn't. Though at two points, Pollock's

soft smile seems inappropriate, the defects are more than compensated by his suave and aquiline walk, by his dignity as old Vallière, and by the caressing, moulding, gestures with which he coaxes a living dove from the empty air.

Fradetal's photography evokes the orthochromatic photography of Feuillade's time without accepting its limitations. In 1917, European film-makers had hardly responded to Griffith's editing innovations, and held, if not to a proscenium effect, at least to a certain framed quality as compared to a camera which Griffith-style, weaves analytically in and out of the action. Franju's scenic sense and his tendency to dramatic detachment both paraphrase features of the archaic idiom, especially when reinforced by an orthochromatic tonality.

One of his film's aesthetic delicacies therefore is the constant interplay between its absolutely modern fluidity, texture and syntax, and archaic evocations which never become quotations because they are thoroughly homogenous with Franju's style. There's nothing far-fetched about this affinity. For Franju's style directly continues the tradition of Murnau, which, with a very deliberate smoothness, counterpoints sustained movement of elements in the shot with movements of the camera and with fluid cutting between shots. The sense of movement in the shot Murnau shared with his German contemporaries of the early 'twenties; it is the kind of movement of which one becomes most conscious in preGriffith syntax. Murnau pioneered elaborate camera-movements, notably in *The Last Laugh* (1925). After Eisenstein's bombshell of the Odessa Steps, he integrated these elements with fast cutting to create an orchestration of movement which is a secret of his films' sustained lyrical power, and makes him one of the masters of cinema. If one doubts whether Franju's films are in the Murnau tradition, the answer is to take one and watch it silent, forgetting the story and concerning oneself simply with the directorial 'choreographics': the way in which, for example, the movement of an object past a motionless camera is continued by the movement of a camera past motionless objects (so that apparently sedentary scenes continue the flow of the action scenes), or the way actors move round and past one another in space. It seems absurd to have to say so, in 1967, but such details of style are not merely details, not 'mere style', not mere ornament. The cinema's visual rhythms are as radical and evocative as the rhythms of poetry or music.

Franju's first creative 'collaboration' with Feuillade occurred in 1938, when he prepared a soundtrack for the showing of *Fantomas* at the Cinémathèque Française. Instead of adding the appropriate noises to the screen action, the obvious possibility, he counterpointed the action with sound. For example, the famous 'choreographic' gunfight around the dockside barrels was overlaid with the sound of a ship's siren. And on reflection it can be seen that this allows the screen action to remain silent, while introducing a new dimension of background, of space. It also counterpoints the dramatic with the scenic. And it avoids a matter-of-fact tautology. For what you see you can't hear, what you hear you can't see. The world is a *little* unreal. The pattern of silence in *Judex* is very Bressonian, and the music is 'a mixture of Jarre's melody and "composed noise".'

As for dialogue, Franju has declared that, if he were his films' dialoguist, all his films would be silent, and it seems that there are, per foot of film, more words in Feuillade's subtitles than in Franju's near-silent talkie. Jacques Champreux (Feuillade's grandson) has said 'We couldn't develop each situation at such length as Feuillade. So the dialogue is conspicuously utilitarian. When Vallière tells Jacqueline, "Your father was the scoundrel which Judex's

letters describe" she hasn't time to wax indignant: she simply says, "Show me proof." It's the actors who confer on the text any richness it may have.'

In other words, we are again in the presence of that withdrawal from the obvious course of a scene which is the technique, not only of Franju, but of Bresson, of Godard (as innumerable statements by him have made absolutely plain), and, for that matter, of Howard Hawks. Champreux's reason for brevity may seem a totally inartistic utilitarianism. But we know how, in any medium, limitations can become inspirations. And to show that the transition from the one to the other may be perfectly natural and perfectly conscious, let us cite the procedure of a director whose cultural background is considerably less sophisticated than Franju's. Asked about his penchant for fast, no-nonsense, under-emotional playing, Hawks replied:

'As far as speed is concerned, I was trained in the old two-reel comedy school, where all we were after was speed. People seemed to like it. so I thought, why not play all comedy fast.'
This rapidity is a natural twin of a dry, understated style:
'Sternberg . . . blows up a little bit of a thing into a great big situation, and I take a great big situation and play it way down. . . . And I think you get a sigh of relief from an audience when they see a familiar old situation come up and you don't bore them with it—just hit it and go on.'
And so in drama as in comedy:
'In *Only Angels Have Wings*, I had a man talking to his friend who's been in an aeroplane wreck, just say to him, "Your neck is broken, kid." Just a flat statement; just try to keep things from becoming mawkish. Play against it completely.'
Thus, the 'utilitarian' avoidance of the obvious dramatic value leads directly to Hawks'

laconism and stoicism, just as a Godard who wasn't detached from his characters wouldn't be Godard. All these years, of course, supposedly sophisticated film reviewers have been assuming that film directors are far too primitive to conceive the idea of playing against a scene, that if Hawks was so curt it must be because he didn't know how to make a scene moving.

So with Franju. Jacqueline's mistrust is too obvious, too foreseeable, to be interesting, and if it's more than indicated, it becomes irrelevant to the film's poetic idiom. Since Franju's and Edith Scob's Jacqueline is tremulously alive as a personality, we don't need psychological verisimilitude to convince us of her reality in depth. What the absence of indignation suggests is that she has long had her own, unspoken misgivings about her father's moral character, and that she is ready to accept it, sad as it makes her, if she can be convinced of it by reason. She thus becomes an intriguingly docile character— first to Favraux's possessiveness, and now to Vallière's moral authority. But she is also ethically strong and prepared to face the truth.

If that exegesis seems far-fetched to some, perhaps the testimony of a no-nonsense, Hollywood artist-craftsman-entertainer should prove indicative: Hawks again: 'The average movie talks too much; you have to make your scenes and plant them and then let the audience do a little work so they become part of it. Any script that *reads* well is no good. If you have to read it three times to understand it, you've got a chance of getting a movie out of it.' That's how good entertainment movies work. Are we to refuse such subtlety to a poet? *Judex* is not a script to *read*, but a movie to *see*.

Another amiable little example of dialogue simplicity: Judex sends Cocantin to telephone for help: 'Call No. 3 at Loisy.' Cocantin goes off, repeating it to himself assiduously, so that he won't forget it. The simple joke is doubly nostalgic. In our era of four-figure numbers the number 3 is as endearingly archaic as a de Dion Bouton. But as Cocantin struggles to remember it, we're reminded of our struggles to memorise four-finger numbers. Cocantin, like Diane at the window, like the film's style, is the past in the present, or the past in its future.

If that detail seems an accidental felicity, there can be nothing accidental in the scene where, before embarking on a car-chase at nightfall, the characters pause to light the wick in the car's paraffin lamps—a detail so realistic yet touching as to be a quiet, tender little surprise. The difference between a poet's approach to serial iconography, and a craftsman's, is indicated by a comparison of *Judex* either with André Hunebelle's *Fantomas* remake, or with Jacques Becker's *Les Aventures d'Arsène Lupin*. Descending the scale, there are also comparisons with any of the recent American recreations of Jules Verne, whose appeal is that of a future-conditional-in-the-impossible (a Victorian moon-rocket, a Great Exhibition-era submarine, and so on).

As the film proceeds, it seems to allude to various other Franju films. From *Les Yeux sans Visage*: the cemetery scenes; Edith Scob hearing her 'dead' father's voice over the 'phone (as in the earlier film Edith Scob's fiancé hears *her* 'dead' voice over the 'phone); the dogs who rescue Edith Scob (as a *quid pro quo* for her freeing them from Genessier's cages?). From *Le Grand Méliès* come Judex's conjuring, and his cinematic inventions (Art Nouveau TV), from *Notre Dame* the pigeon dead on the balcony, with the old bullnose automobiles for lumbering barges. Even more uncanny: several of these details (notably the hounds) are in Feuillade's *Judex* too, and the knowledgeable spectator of Franju's film has an eerie sensation, as two cinematographic eras merge.

Franju's film was programmed at the Paris-Pullman, with Robbe-Grillet's first directorial effort, *L'Immortelle*. Robbe-Grillet, had by then reacted against his earlier exclusion of subjectivity from realism, and lurched to the equal absurdity whereby subjectivity is the only realism. He set out to create a work of art which, because it doesn't claim to be 'realistic' (i.e. a re-creation of some 'other' world) can make the fullest possible use of its own reality, creating impossible, or mutually contradictory, or 'riddle' worlds. Yet Franju's film achieves just what Robbe-Grillet's doesn't. It renders credible, and it simultaneously denies, a world in the negative subjunctive, a world which seems tenderly aware of its own unreality. In the cinema as in literature, Robbe-Grillet's dogmatic machines, rendered ineffectual by the simple-minded rigidity of his principles, led to his acceptance, even in England, once the country of common-sense, as an avant-gardist. Yet a film critic still has to labour the point that the director of *Le Sang des Bêtes* has sufficient sophistication to require 'reading between the lines'.

Still: Judex—*the triumph of good.*

Thomas l'Imposteur

Cocteau gave Franju the rights of *Thomas l'Imposteur* in 1952, saying that he'd rather be betrayed by him than by anyone else. First published in 1923, the novel was doubtless suggested by Cocteau's own World War I experiences with a military ambulance and a detachment of Marines. While the Paris *haut monde* prepares to flee before the German onslaught, a French-Polish widow, the Princesse de Bormes, organises an ambulance service to supplement the military effort. Though bitterly resented by the professionals, whose routines she disturbs, she is able to reach the front line thanks to the peculiar charm of a youth who sports a subaltern's uniform and bears the same surname as a popular General. But Thomas is an impostor, and war, whose disorders made his pretence possible, at last imposes its own order on him. Fired at while in No-Man's-Land, he just has time to think 'I must sham dead' before he dies. At last, his reality and fiction have become one.

Years later, Cocteau, with his film *Orphée*, was to recreate his personal myth in terms of secret police, blackouts, midnight interrogations, the whole nightmare atmosphere of the Occupation. In the same way, *Thomas l'Imposteur* is both a grimly oppressive evocation of the horrors of war, and another myth woven from the motifs to which Cocteau has so often turned for inspiration. As Orphée is lured by the poetry which comes to him from the land of death, so Thomas is lured to the great unreality which is war. As Orphée is taken to his death in a Rolls-Royce belonging to his Princess, so Thomas is taken to the front in the ambulance of La Princesse de Bormes. No-Man's-Land prefigures La Zone, whose ruins were those of a military academy. The mirror motif appears: while artillery thunders all along the horizon, Thomas fires at his reflection with a ridiculous little pistol.

Constantly Cocteau returns to comparisons between the theatre of war and theatre in the sense of illusion. The apparently deserted dunes are honeycombed with trenches, and so are 'nothing but tricks, décor, *trompe-l'oeil*, traps and artifice'. The warren of cellars beneath the ruins of Nieuport are compared to the maze of rooms and corridors behind and beneath a theatre-stage. Approaching the front for the first time, the Princess sees soldiers shaving and dressing in the fields, and thinks: 'Ah—the actors are preparing.' After Thomas's part-playing is ended, he is buried in the Marines' Cemetery, a huge bank of sand shaped like a ship—another décor, another lie.

The Princess is accompanied by a sort of parody of herself, Madame Valiche, an ex-actress who raises funds for the war-effort by laying out a mock-up of the front-line trenches in the Princess's grounds. Later, she heads a troupe of actors and entertains the front-line troops with a programme of plays, which itself goes grotesquely wrong: the soldiers imagine they're watching a three-act play, and can't quite follow the plot. In the film, Madame Valiche recites a passage from Edmond Rostand, whose jejune patriotism quite chills the blood. The Princess may have a flair for the theatrical gesture, but hers is the theatricality of life, whereas Madame Valiche's is the vulgar rhetoric of death, her troupe the ultimate insult to dying soldiers.

The theme of truth, deception and self-deception is re-echoed in the personal story. The Princess 'played with life as a virtuoso plays the piano, and turned everything to the same effect which those musicians draw from mediocre music as from the most beautiful'. She is led to her charitable enterprise by a flamboyance which—and here is another deception—conceals the fact that she is a superior, generous soul, 'not afraid of the wrinkles made by smiles'. Without quite realising it, she is in love with Thomas, and Thomas, without quite realising it, loves her daughter Henriette, but mistakes the disquiet which she arouses in him for impatience to experience the war. Henriette loves him, but is too shy to approach him until urged on by, ironically, her mother. The letter in which Henriette tells Thomas the truth about their feelings for each other is assumed at his unit to be an important military message; going to fetch it, he imprudently exposes himself to the 'truthful' light of the flares and is killed.

In Franju's words, 'Thomas isn't Thomas; he's a ghost. The real male star of the film is the war. Sadoul hit on the title which the film should have had: The Great Imposture.' The journalist who loves the Princess fills his newspapers with optimistic sentiments, but privately begs her to flee from Paris, which he is convinced must be lost. When the German push is repelled, he insists: 'I was right in principle; if Paris didn't fall, it was an accident' —a line which is much more than a parody of French intellectuals. Even those who know the truth are trapped in the lies: a telling detail in the film shows an injured soldier limping his way into Madame Valiche's front-line mock-up, and docilely paying his money, while old men, ladies and schoolchildren stroll round the trenches, the snipers' nests, and all the terrain of war, utterly charmed.

These deceptions are echoed in the prestige games which mean more to those in power than the life and death of their men. The authorities, though incapable of providing adequate medical aid for their vast casualties, do everything to frustrate the Princess's private enterprise. And a bishop, mortally offended because the Princess didn't ask his permission before driving her ambulances through the town, refuses to provide her with petrol, though he repents under the charm of Thomas. All these games result from the play of ambition and vanity which has come to masquerade as authority and turns society's official aims into by-products and legal fictions, constituting a massive structure of deceit in which the soldiers are trapped like flies stuck on a web.

The baroque quality of the theatre-war antithesis is enhanced by Cocteau's prose style, itself more baroque than it may appear. It is strange, after all, to find in a grimly realistic war story such imagery as this, of Thomas's strange power of convincing others: 'A special fairy casts this spell at birth. Some succeed, to whose cradle no fairy came but this.' The curious sense of remoteness and unreality, so often attendant on life-and-death situations, makes Cocteau's almost metaphysical sense of life as unreality deceptively true to the subjective reality of war, as when he writes of 'the anti-aircraft guns which crowned the aeroplanes with little ball-shaped clouds, resembling the seraphim around the Holy Virgin'. Cocteau so often applies such delicate feminine metaphors to the harsh masculine realities of war, that more than visual and ecclesiastical associations seem to be aroused when he writes that, after a shattering by shells, 'The cathedral was a mountain of old lace.' Very occasionally, Cocteau slips into sentimentality, as when he says of Thomas, whose other name is Guillaume, 'Guillaume the artificial was without artifice. His intact heart understood depths which his infantile understanding could not probe'—a sentence which jars on me like Pollock's smile in *Judex*. Otherwise, Cocteau's precise, almost brittle style is very much in the terse French tradition to which the nearest English approach is perhaps Rayner Heppenstall's 'Saturnine'. It is also a very oral style: Cocteau spoke as incisively and elegantly as he wrote, and, as Franju remarked, he is a poet whom one sees (in plays or films) or hears (in plays or poems) rather than reads. Cocteau is a perfect refutation of McLuhan's misguided attempt to correlate print culture with a visual culture, for on the page his sentences are so terse and tight that, as the eye runs over them, the ear is forced to hear them. In his novels, people, scenes or events are spared the reams of incidental detail which goes with the written word (as opposed to the spoken word). 'The cathedral was a mountain of old lace' could not be more devoid of emotional words, or of precise information—yet how evocative are those eight words! Where the usual English novelist feels obliged to put all sorts of circumstantial flesh on the bones of his point to give it meaning, to give it vividness and the apparent continuity of lived experience, Cocteau boldly pares down until the scene is reduced to an anecdote. Only the original French can do justice to the crispness of rhythm, of sound, of idea: '*La veille, a l'hôpital, on venait d'apprendre à un artilleur qu'il fallait lui couper la jambe sans chloroforme, que c'était la seule chance de le sauver, et il fumait, blême, une dernière cigarette avant le supplice, lorsqu'un obus réduisit le matériel chirurgical en poudre, et tua deux aides-majors. Personne n'osa reparaître devant l'artilleur. On dût laisser la gangrène l'envahir comme le lierre une statue.*'

That artilleryman lacks a face, an age, an original human touch, a personal identity, everything which, according to the commonest assumptions of English literary theory, is needed to make a scene real for a reader. This English approach might be described as neo-cinematographic, in that it wants everything to be made into a scene which is going on, so to speak, before and around the reader, a scene for the eye and, of course, the other senses too. It even underlies the English emphasis on metaphor—everything is made into a picture of a physical equivalent. And it underlies the sillier English theories of cinema, according to which the content of a movie is 'literary', i.e. the sort of scene that an English novelist would find it easy to describe in words. But theories of literature as scene, though useful within a certain area (particularly nineteenth-century novels and poems) are inadequate for literature as a whole, for literature is basically a matter of words and of ideas, and whether or not these ideas fall into a scenic continuity is a purely secondary distinction. Paradox and apothegm, for example, are non-scenic continuities; the anecdote is a non-scenic narrative form, like the story of the artilleryman above—a story whose vividness lies in the tension of ideas. Because Cocteau uses so few words, every word can have a full weight of meaning, given a careful choice and arrangement. In a fashionable formulation, one can say that 'less is more'. Because Cocteau says so little, the comparison between gangrene climbing up a leg and ivy climbing up a statue has its full effect, its extremely cruel irony. It isn't really a metaphor so much as an anti-metaphor, for the living ivy is external to the durable stone, while gangrene is internal to the soft corruptible flesh.

In a sense, Cocteau's is a very non-cinematographic prose-style. A minor problem for those of us who believe that style reveals the workings of the mind is that the visual style of Cocteau's films, for which he is quite certainly as responsible as his photographers and art directors, is completely different from his prose style. In

Still: Thomas l'Imposteur. *Fabrice Rouleau as Thomas.*

influence is a unique mind). But Cocteau had also seen Mack Sennett, Westerns, and *Battleship Potemkin*, and was profoundly affected by *Le Sang des Bêtes*. Why did he choose to absorb the expressionistic idiom when he might instead have responded to any of the innumerable cinematographic styles which correspond to his prose, or which he could easily have adapted to correspond to his prose? The answer is, perhaps, that Cocteau used movies to express another side of his mind, a side which appears less in the text than in the underlying mood of such plays as *L'Aigle à Deux Têtes* and *Les Parents Terribles*. Cocteau used movies for the common, absolutely legitimate and, by modern trends, slightly naive purpose of plunging himself into words of nightmare or magic, or of reality experienced with the global quality of a nightmare—a state to which his autobiographic writing regularly alludes, but from which his prose takes a detachment which is at once dandyish, stoic and ironic. His prose is that of an expert skater tracing lines on the glittering surface of the ice—his films move through the dark cold waters beneath. His films *immerse* one, his prose is a tracery of paradoxes. Each medium fills out the other, and Cocteau, as one would expect from an artist working in so many media, cannot be understood fully through any one medium.

This versatility, as Franju observes, can be something of a problem for his would-be adaptor. In filming a Cocteau novel, is the appropriate style Cocteau's dandyism or his expressionism? In adapting *Les Enfants Terribles*, Jean-Pierre Melville adopted the last course; Cocteau, with *Le Testament d'Orphée*, seemed to be fumbling for a dandyish treatment of motifs previously filmed in an expressionist style. Cocteau's verbal style is clearly contrary to the temperament of Franju, for whom poetry and magic are, so to speak, an extreme possibility: one of the poles of human thought,

Franju's words, 'Cocteau's cinematographic style, whose roots are in German expressionism which he liked very much, a style which looks to mythology for symbols with contemporary extensions, is the contrary of his written style which is light, musical, decorative, very French, and whose ornament occasionally camouflages the meaning.' Are we to conclude from this that, as some art historians argue, style is a matter only, or largely, of influence, that Cocteau's written style was formed by French prose, whereas his cinematographic style resulted from the best movies which he happened to see, and has no connection with the literary part of his mind?

Clearly, no-one's style is exempt from influences (although there must surely be a non-anonymous stylistic element, since the closest rather than, as for Cocteau, more real than a life which, alas, was less real than illusion and death. Franju, who has a tender heart, never betrays an author wantonly, through indifference or ignorance of his intentions; he betrays deliberately, and he betrays minimally, just enough to be true to his own vision. And what he has seen in Cocteau's novel is, not simply a contradiction of Cocteau's vision, but a complement to it.

Franju doesn't just immerse one in realism, and adopt a more detached but still sympathetic attitude to those who are, like the Princess and Thomas, 'merely players'. Cocteau himself writes in a very detached way about his heroes. His affinity with them is revealed only by his fascination with them, by their position as the most generous characters in the film, and by the absence of any more valid or viable attitude. One might expect Franju to moralise in Sartrean style at the expense of their 'false consciousness', their frivolous counterfeit of commitment, their substitution of the poverty of imagination and self-dramatisation for the profundity of real involvement, and so on. There are certainly undertones of that in Franju's film, as we shall see. But since Franju, nearer Freud than Sartre, sees consciousness as a compromise between fantasy and reality anyway, he's not so concerned with what could easily become a 'fundamentalist' moral position. Franju no more condemns the Princess and Thomas than he condemns Gérane in *La Tête contre les Murs*. If we don't condemn the mad, why condemn the half-mad or the sane? One simply notes the consequences of their behaviour for them and for others. The element of integrity in madness is stranger and more interesting than its deviation from outer reality.

In his sympathy with Cocteau, Franju departs sharply from the Surrealist party line. For the Surrealists, Cocteau was something of a *bête-noire*, his similarity with them (his respect for the dream-life) only serving to exacerbate the contradictions. Cocteau was always a darling of the social and literary salons which they loathed. He never took the step from criticising society to revolting against it, but seemed to prefer a kind of pessimistic acquiescence, which led to a distinctly unfortunate gesture during the Occupation. And the pederastic 'martyrdom', of which he made no particular secret, struck the Surrealists, who were rather illogically puritanical about pederasty, as more a repression of libido than an assertion of it, which perhaps in his case (as opposed to the sodomitical ruminations of Sade) it probably was. To them, any nonconformism by Cocteau would be only a lapdog's yap, and, of course, he did conclude by carrying, beautifully, the sword of the Immortals of the Académie Française, a sword perhaps not so different from the sabres which, in *Hôtel des Invalides*, light the way to Paradise.

This hostility can be justified in terms of *Thomas l'Imposteur*. One of its rebels against society's system is a beautiful aristocratic hostess, who would enjoy all sorts of privileges anyway, and has no hesitation here in making the most of them for herself and her friends. She's splendidly convinced she can't be harmed, so her Florence Nightingale act isn't at all sacrificial. The other rebel is a boy who, far from trying to get away from the butchery, is so taken by its glamour that he sacrifices himself to it. It's true that Cocteau sees the boy's end as tragic, but in Cocteau tragedy tends to be acquiescent, fatalistic, even masochistic (*Orphée* is distinctly masochistic), rather than being pitched in the key of rebellion, accusation and anger. In *Thomas l'Imposteur*, death is represented, not by a menacing but attractive woman, but by the system of war, a vast, impersonal slaughterhouse. Nonetheless, the war as it fascinates and draws him, is, in a dream sense, a 'male star', the neo-realistic equivalent of La Bête in *La Belle et La Bête*, drawing its terrified victims towards it. However, in its more public reference, the story reads as an indictment of systematised madness, losing an ambivalence which is more private to Cocteau. Thomas's fascination with war can be used to dismiss him, but it is in itself tragic: 'those whom the authorities would destroy, they first make mad'. To make mad is, in this sense, to blind to reality. Thomas is as truly an innocent as Edith Scob slaughtering birds in *Thérèse Desqueyroux*, as, in another way, Judex. He is pure enough to matter. And Franju's film makes quite clear what is more ambiguous in the novel: the Princess, though not destroyed, is defeated by the vast machine.

At times, Franju and Cocteau seem gracefully to change roles: Cocteau describes a wounded horse turning the corner of a road, limping in its own hanging intestines; Franju paraphrases it by the more dreamlike image of a horse, neighing in terror, galloping through the ruins with flames streaming from its mane. Indeed most of the points which an incautious *auteur* theory would ascribe to Franju, are from Cocteau: the bishop who won't give petrol for the ambulance, the priest forcing a tetanus-locked mouth open with a penknife so as to insert the Host, the unapproachable artilleryman. Still, *auteur* theory may not be so wrong after all; another director could also select, or evolve from Cocteau's novel, those details which are him, and not Franju at all. (It would make an interesting exercise for student scriptwriters: 'Without inventing anything, prepare an adaptation of Cocteau's novel for any one of the following: a) Jean-Luc Godard, b) King Vidor, c) G. W. Pabst, d) Andrzej Wajda.') More obviously Cocteau-like is Franju's use of reflections. It's true they're absent in the novel, but they are probably keyed by Franju's knowledge of Cocteau's films, and by the scene where Thomas, near gunfire, raises his revolver at arm's length to fire into his own reflection, rather like Orphée extending his magic-gloved hand through a mirror beyond which lies the Zone. There is a scattering of images in which windows are used as mirrors (notably, the breathtaking shot of shellbursts on the horizon reflected in a car window beyond which the Princess stares at them with quiet horror). Cocteau's sense of life and theatre as mirrors facing each other is, of course, a Franjuvian theme too, determining, as we have seen, the structure of *Le T.N.P.* The difference is that, while Cocteau uses it to query the reality of life, to suggest that dream and reality converge only at a point beyond the death of the life-force, Franju uses it to assert the reality of art, to suggest that dream is the heightening of

Still: Thomas l'Imposteur.

129

reality by life. Cocteau, too, has commented on the similarities between magic, poetry and conjuring, similarities implicit in the final image of Judex, Jacqueline and the dove.

Where Cocteau leaves the artilleryman vague, and Franju incarnates the characters, the film must alter the emphasis. Cocteau describes war by means of ideas of theatre and trickery; the military reality becomes an aspect of metaphysical deceit. Franju makes concrete the forms from which the themes of theatricality and trickery emerge. In Cocteau, the material details, while cuttingly critical of society, are *examples* of the profound, almost metaphysical deceptions which he sees everywhere, in family life, in poetry, in fairy-stories, in myth. With Franju's inflexibly materialistic style, the trickery is a function of society, a maze in which the Princess and Thomas are hopelessly lost, against which each opposes his own fiction. The fictions are less hollow because they are expressions of their own choices, not passive responses to social pressures, but they are nonetheless a failure to see life steadily and to see life whole.

For this reason, the loss of a metaphysical plane is not an impoverishment. In the novel, the metaphysical theme deprives the realistic level of its fullest intensity. Bitter as it is, Cocteau's novel made little or no impact, until Franju's film came along. In Franju, the metaphysical level is cut off until the last shot, and the interplay of ironies is concentrated and intensified, just as waves are reflected back by the sides of a cup. If Cocteau's novel inspires anger, it also inspires acceptance of Thomas's death as a fulfilment of destiny. Franju's film inspires anger at society, and pity, but Thomas's death is simply the end of a process into which he has been lured. As so often in Franju, the spectator's consciousness of time past becomes part of the film. 'The actors are dressing,' thinks the Princess. But we, in 1967, know all

about the slaughter of the trenches, a slaughter which has for us a nostalgic fascination. She has yet to learn what haunts us like a race-memory; we wait for her to experience a shock on which we look back. Her ignorance is an irony, it enhances, by contrast, our pain (as the idea of ivy round stone enhances our idea of poison in flesh).

Because Franju is refusing Cocteau's implication that all life is illusion, the possibility of really experiencing external reality brings out another theme, which is latént in the novel, and affords another similarity between Franju and Resnais. *Hiroshima Mon Amour* is the story of Riva's attempt to get to Hiroshima to grasp the event of 1945; if she had been there, she would have been only on the remote fringes of the event, because otherwise she would now be dead. Thomas, too, is seeking to grasp the atrocities of World War I. He still hasn't found the reality that kills him. The Princess is seeking to affirm her life in the face of death. But in the gutted town, she encounters the shattered remnants of a mother and daughter, who might have been herself and her daughter. And because she loves her daughter, she feels through the calcined corpses, she *sees* war. To the '*Non, tu n'as rien vu à Hiroshima*' of Resnais and Duras, one can oppose '*Non, tu n'as rien vu à Reims.*' But Franju, unlike Cocteau, is a realist: knowing is possible; and unlike Duras, there is no solipsism in Franju; knowing is possible, without dying, through that identification with victims which is the root and crux of Franju's art.

The Princess's insight echoes an earlier scene, where a German doctor in an ill-lit stable has to decide rapidly which of his injured men are well enough to be worth moving. Shrugging, he jabs each one in the pile with a pitchfork; if they are well enough to leap up in pain, then they have a chance of surviving the jolting voyage in the ambulance. This is know-

ing, military style, without love. This doctor has seen everything at Reims, and nothing.

Having seen war, the Princess does not return to the front. In a sense, she dwindles, like Judex, steadily throughout the picture. At the ball with which it opens, she alone shines, opposing that brilliant optimism, that flair for the reckless gesture, so typical of the Polish aristocracy, to the ashamed gloom of the French—a jealous girl promptly concludes she's a spy. Whether or not one bears in mind the history of the Polish aristocracy—so often crushed by the Germans, the Russians, and the

Still: Thomas l'Imposteur. *Emmanuele Riva and Fabrice Rouleau among the casualties.*

peasantry which in its turn it exploited, but always undeterred—the contrast between the romantic Princess and the pessimistic, rationalist journalist is another aspect of the dream-reality dichotomy. But, after her flying start, she is unable to deal with officialdom. It is Madame Valiche, by her blend of crude rhetoric and sense of army realities, or it is Thomas, by his 'connections' and his charm, who get the ambulances through. Even then, they are

131

allowed to pick up only the wounded whom official channels would rather not have, that is, the badly wounded who probably won't survive anyway. Finally, the Princess confronts the bodies and thereafter does her Florence Nightingale act back in her own mansion. Is there a streak of cowardice in her response, a fear of seeing her own elegant, lively body shattered like the peasant's? Perhaps; why not? In an age where right- and left-wing alike vie with each other in conscripting and controlling the individual to square with their ideological and administrative problems, with their economic or moral dogmas, with jingoisms of country or class, then of course an emotion as sensible as self-preservation will be reviled as cowardice. There's no room for Falstaffs in the twentieth century. In a sense, the film Franju hasn't yet made is the story of a male equivalent of the Princess, the story of a deserter, of a man who withdraws himself from a war for no other reason than that he doesn't care who wins, and finds his own side just as dangerous as the other. Claude Autant-Lara has made the companion-piece, *Tu ne tueras point*, about conscientious objection, still hardly recognised outside Great Britain and America. And a similarly 'isolationist' attitude underlies both King Vidor's *The Big Parade* and *War and Peace*, the first of which is very far from being the simple epic of World War I which it may appear to be.

The Princess has a second motive, perhaps more moral, perhaps less robust: a noble disgust at a system which she realises herself powerless to affect. Not that she becomes irresponsible; after four o'clock tea, she changes from her fur and ostrich feathers into a nurse's uniform, which is plain, but becoming. She allows Madame Valiche to use her grounds for a patriotic bazaar although she herself has seen the truth of the war. She connives. She becomes an eclipsed character, and it is the boy

who goes off to suffer the war for himself. She weeps at the station like a war widow because, in a way which is half-woman, half-mother, she loves him, but has become utterly powerless, just a war widow.

Nor is she immune from the fate she flees. Deserted by Thomas, who returns to the front, Henriette languishes, falls ill, and poisons herself. In the novel, the misunderstood letter hardly relates to society; it is a machination by fate, like the letters which cross in *Les Enfants Terribles*. Given Franju's emphasis on the social system, the separation and the letter are the corollaries of Thomas's decision to return to the front, i.e. of being a victim of mystification. The war reached out and killed her just as dead as if she were a battlefield corpse, and it kills Thomas too. And the Princess? No doubt, after November 11, 1918, she will join in the general rejoicing, and become a luminary of the frivolous 'twenties.

This theme is unfolded in Franju's characteristically tight-lipped way. At a first viewing, it might seem that, for him, the civilian theme is present only as an ironic contrast to the 'film within the film': the front line sequences. But this would be to miss that sense of networks which recurs in his films—networks of the city in *Le Sang des Bêtes*, of reality and illusion in *Le T.N.P.*, of time in *Thérèse Desqueyroux*, of irreality in *Judex*. Emmanuele Riva endows Polish exuberance with all her French finesse; the interplay between this devastatingly imperious and sensitive woman, and Franju's dour, detached style, is of a contrariness so extreme, yet so fascinating, that one hardly knows whether one's dissatisfaction or one's fascination is the sharper response. As in *Thérèse Desqueyroux*, one wishes that the camera, instead of watching the Riva character, would more often allow her to dominate the camera, to burst out of her place in the composition, to flood us with her emotion. And this is something which Franju never allows, except perhaps in the ball scene, where anyway she dominates the scene of which she is part. The reason here is only secondarily a matter of camera-angle or camera-distance; the real issue is the restraint placed by Franju on his actors. It's not that their parts, or their performances, are in any sense underdeveloped; everything is indicated, but so quietly and briefly compared to the usual rise and fall of emotion even in films as sophisticated as *Hiroshima Mon Amour*, that one is left slightly let down, puzzled perhaps, and has to see the film again, bearing in mind that what at first seemed merely a prelude is also, within, a climax. Edith Scob is so immediately magic a character that her mere appearance is itself a climax; from Emmanuele Riva one expects a certain flow which Franju (unlike Resnais) does not quite allow. Edith Scob's mere appearance is in itself a complex statement; one wants to meditate over it. Emmanuele Riva's is also a question; one longs to trace the evolution of her moods. The film would have been more immediately appealing as a dramatic unity had the turbulence of her responses been more fully shared, instead of merely indicated. But detachment, in some form or another, is, as we shall see in discussing some strange aspects of the film's style, a precondition of Franju's approach.

A similar distance obtains between the spectator and Thomas. Cocteau makes no attempt to depict, or account for Thomas's charm, telling us he had it, and through metaphors persuading us that it really is something magic. Franju has avoided the incarnation of Thomas which would most surely involve an audience in his fate. This would be to give him something of Rupert Brooke; to endow him with an obvious sensitivity, charm and dreaminess, to wring the maximum contrast from his apparent social origin and his actual one, from

his gallantry to Henriette and the Princess and his fascination with war, from his promise and his death. Franju shows us a Thomas who is slightly inadequate, distinctly withdrawn, rather expressionless, whose charm remains, to this critic at least, invisible. If Franju places his seduction of the bishop off-screen, he is rigorously following Cocteau. Nonetheless, one longs to know how he softened the other (without trying), and, for that matter, how the other softened. In the exchange which we do see, the softening of the senior officer who bawls him out seems to come from the officer's possession of a certain good nature, which is unexpected under the cantankerous military face. It is as if Franju set out to make Thomas a ghost, the ghost, perhaps, of male vulnerability in a world geared to hierarchies, orders and slaughter. Because his uncle is a popular general, people can allow themselves to respond to the boy, to become, for a moment, human again; how agreeable, after all, to satisfy, by one concession, one's kindliness, one's lick-spittle tendencies, one's romanticism and one's nostalgias for youth.

But Thomas struck me at least as spoiled rather than vulnerable, as petulant rather than sensitive. Maybe Franju preferred to key Thomas's appearance to his inadequacy, in a sense, his stupidity, to keep it in our minds, and to play it off against the opinions other people have of him, to make of him something which would be derisive if it weren't so sadly typical of the young. He's a ghost because he has been taken over by all the banal notions of the glamour and manliness of war, he has been caught by his very innocence; in short, he's an adolescent idiot who'd probably have been very happy sharing the rough male kiss of blankets along with all the rest of the Hitler Jugend, or whatever its French equivalent was. Yet one can't but understand, pity and admire the boy. His relationship with the Marines, which is very true, emerges in the dialogue but hardly in the images, perhaps because Franju is anxious to avoid the romanticism of camaraderie and the handsome young warrior image. Nonetheless, Franju's penchant for restraint and ellipse seems to me to have resulted in miscasting and perhaps misdirection here. For all that, Thomas comes vividly right during an interlude in his masquerade, when after drinking too much he awakes, hung-over, in his lower-middle-class adolescent bedroom, to whine to and be nursed by the old aunt with whom he lives.

Cocteau remarked to Franju: 'I write, you show.' This refers to a distinction of style, not of media. For in the cinema showing is writing, and how you say it is what you say about it. The translatability of *mise-en-scène* into philosophy is classically demonstrated when, a few seconds after the burning horse has shrieked by, a fire-engine tears along in the distance. But it won't be for the horse. The contrast is exactly equivalent to the 'Yes, but . . .' construction which Buñuel adopted for *Las Hurdes*. A construction which is dramatic in Buñuel becomes scenic in Franju (but the scenic is also dramatic). The same reversal occurs in the astonishing shot inside the burning house, with the door clapping, sparks showering, and quivering shadows emphasising the jolting of the entire structure, endowing it, and the fire, with life. The detail of flames bursting through a girl's portrait is not a new idea, but the actual physical details of the burning are effectively hideous in suggestion. After Payot's death by an enemy bullet, when Roy, jokingly, shines a torch in his face, Roy's slow decline is paraphrased by a classic cinematic economy. Thomas says: 'It was a stray bullet . . .' and Roy responds by turning the torch up to shine on his own face. The fear there gives the expiatory act an altruistic rigour which mere toughness could never possess. We

are, perhaps, disappointed, as Roy is, when no bullet answers from the darkness, to take the weight from his mind. And the gesture crystallises, in an extreme and black form, the virile love which Cocteau only states and which Franju, otherwise, understates.

The opening ball is the twin of that in *Judex*, but not an identical one. Each couple spins stiffly in its own little circle, while, beyond, the bows of the violinists strike down as stiffly as swords. Under this opulent panoply, society conceals its fear, but the result of their stalemate is a state of living deadness akin to *Marienbad*, and better anchored in human experience. Constantly Franju indulges a quietly virtuoso placing of movement in depth. In the interiors, our eye is led from the dancing couples in the foreground to the line of violin bows, above their heads, beyond. Intricate yet rigid patterns on wallpaper, curtains, and bedsteads, draw the eye to them, invest them with a silent tension. Yet, unlike the analogous effects in Dreyer's *Vampyr*, the result is not one of flatness; the rooms retain a kind of glittering volume, at once soft-textured and sharp-edged, sumptuous and funereal. At times the sense of planes is as vehement as it is in Murnau's *Nosferatu*, which is possibly the first film in which the pattern of visual space is 'laminated' into real or implied planes. Particularly ghostly, in its enigmatic way, is the camera's rapid track towards a window which, because it gives on to the night, is glistening black. But, as the camera penetrates it, the scene suddenly lights up to show a beautiful carriage in the drive beyond, where guests are departing. The effect, jarring with its mixture of perceptual literalism and unreality, is of an abrupt presence, as of living ghosts, of ghosts-in-waiting, in a word, of the end of an epoch.

In its picture of the front line, the film is nearer Pabst's *Westfront* 1918 than Milestone's *All Quiet on the Western Front*: the mood is not

134

of hectic slaughter so much as of slow, oppressive attrition. The personal story and the larger canvas are impeccably welded by the simplest, most effective, and least used cinematic means: control over space-in-depth. Franju's screen is infinitely larger than CinemaScope, because of his visual sense. Again and again, a detail isolated on or near the horizon—perhaps one moving lorry, perhaps mist—draws our eye out across desolate space, evokes the whole tentacular functioning of the system, and reminds us of death proceeding nearby, maybe over the next ridge. The next effect will seem absurdly forced to all those who don't wish to understand that cinematic style is as much a matter of control over the spectator's visual *Gestalt* as all the other visual arts, as much a matter of control over detail. The camera pans to follow a truck; the shot of the truck yields little information, and we allow ourselves to be distracted and fix on something visually more active, interesting; the rough skyline of a bank running along above the road. The bank abruptly ends, and our eye, continuing its trajectory, shoots out across a vast plain unfolding below.

In a night scene, a patch of torn bark on a tree-trunk catches the light. It is in the foreground to the main action, but surrounded on the screen by an area which is in the background to the action. Thus, suddenly, space is tightened, environment wrapped round the people, isolating and imprisoning them. In other cases, the linkage is dramatically more direct, like the shot of the indignant Bishop, framed in the little rear window of the ambulance, and emphasized by being a small receding picture in a black surround (a similar effect is obtained, with a church-front, during Thérèse's car-ride). Nor could war's strange ability to seem both remote and ubiquitous be better suggested than by one or two enigmatic interlacings between the war-machine and our friends. Riders with rudimentary gas-masks urge their horses towards a vast, semi-permanent gas-cloud, lying low over the fields like mist. Proud, erect, anonymous cavalrymen ride by; one falls.

Franju's style is compositionally too tense to catch Cocteau's sense of war as *désordre*, though there is a delightful approximation to it when the commentary likens the Princess's house to a Ministry, and the image shows papers, too hurriedly packed in the panic of evacuation, being blown chaotically in every direction by the wind, like, perhaps, the birds of madness.

The disassociation of commentary and image is taken to its furthest point outside Bresson and Godard. The episode of the gangrenous artilleryman is little more than a tableau; the image is, in a sense, only an accompaniment for the commentary, rather than the other way round. A tourist's eye at the foot of the bed would see only a silent, glowering face, the horror is in the ineloquence of seen reality. Later the commentary explains that for Thomas the music of a passing Algerian regiment is eerie and magical. The camera shows only tired men; here, reality grimly refuses to accommodate the fantasies of the romantic little fellow, nor is he allowed to communicate to us a wonderment which we would be as foolish as he is to share. Franju is interested in the boy who has the illusions, but he is not interested in his illusions; they must be stated, but we must continue to be conscious of reality, of what he forgets or can't see. In the discrepancy between the two lies the horror. Here, perhaps, is Franju's deliberate betrayal of Cocteau, the betrayal which Cocteau anticipated, and maybe felt he deserved, as a punishment for his masochistic dreams. Did Cocteau see in Franju's sympathetic but rigorous materialism the satisfaction of the longing which *Le Testament d'Orphée*, a film about

Cocteau as Cocteau, so wistfully concludes?

Franju for his part pays Cocteau a final compliment which is so gently back-handed it's a nostalgic caress. Thomas dies as a spray of flares blossoms in the night sky; the camera tracks past them and through the stars, one of which becomes Cocteau's symbol. It's a *faux-naif* effect—the reference is not only to Cocteau, but to another magician-conjurer, Georges Méliès, whose films so often included trips to charmingly unrealistic planets and whose firm was in fact called Star Films. If that association seems forced, the short answer is Franju's own description of the scene as 'a fairy-story expansion of the décor—"an apotheosis", as Méliès used to say'. The nostalgic Pirandellism which never lies far from Franju's mind (being a simple extension of his detachment: if from the characters, why not from the film?) appears also in the choice of commentator. As he chose the author of *Thérèse* for *Thérèse*, so he chooses Jean Marais, who played so many of Cocteau's heroes, notably, of course, Orphée. The effect isn't altogether successful, in detail: Marais skilfully imitates the delivery of his old friend, but his gruffer voice hasn't the extraordinary flute-rapier finesse of the poet's. In the context of Cocteau's preoccupation with death, false death and death-in-death as resurrection, the idea of a posthumous author's commentary is a beautiful one.

In *Films and Filming* Peter Whitehead points out that the novel is concerned 'with the first signs of that disassociation that is still with us', that Godard's *Le Petit Soldat* contains a reference to Thomas's death (which is already pure Godard, even down to its facetious punning), and that Thomas might well be described as *Le Petit Soldat*, frivolously engaging himself in a torture-machine which destroys him. In Franju's rather dour refusal to entertain Thomas's illusions there is, perhaps, an equivalent of the Marxist hard-headedness which underlies Brecht's theory of alienation effects. Without discussing the theory's pros and cons, one finds something analogous to it in the films made in Italy by the flood of intellectual young Marxists since the governmental 'opening to the left' removed the previously crippling censorship. Close-ups are used sparingly, characters are constantly kept in their social context, the spectator sees what they feel but isn't encouraged to feel what they feel; there are principal characters, but nothing like the perspective of heroism and identification which makes so many American films so jejune. Franju seems less concerned with the social context *per se* than with an implacable insistence on the tragedies which *are*.

Implacable, yet tender; violent, yet nostalgic; beautiful, but sullen; well-made, by traditional canons, but drastically aware of art-forms and memory-forms as merely forms: the products of Franju's inspiration are sparked by its inner contradictions, by the energy of opposite poles. He has created the most tough-minded of documentaries, and a fairy-tale conjuring up *temps-perdu* with a smooth elegance worthy of Max Ophuls, like whom he has a magic touch with period ballrooms. Yet the diverse elements and attitudes are so perfectly fused that, however often one sees his films, one can't see *through* them, however minutely their forms are analysed by the mind's eye (words are too clumsy), their mood can't be analysed away. Like many films whose complexity is covert, they may at first viewing seem merely mood pieces, given a sharper aesthetic pleasure by Franju's skill in evading ideological censorships. But they look perhaps a little too restrained in style, a little limited in range. Only with second and third viewings, do the full complexity and real meanings of the films begin to emerge and their real power to be perceived.

Les Rideaux Blancs

When, earlier, we contrasted *le regard* of Franju, which has behind it the complexity and balance of the artistic mainstream, with *le regard* of the *nouveau roman*, which so constantly yields to all the temptations to monomania that beset *avant-gardes*, we may have seemed to be wandering from our brief. But it is in the nature of the mainstream to incorporate innovations into itself, and so it is none too surprising that the alienating eye of Franju should reveal its affinities-by-opposition with the *nouveau roman*. The negative subjunctive of *Judex* contrasts with that of Robbe-Grillet's *L'Immortelle*. With *Les Rideaux Blancs*, originally an episode for a French TV film devoted to *L'Instant de la Paix*, Franju turns to a scenario by Marguerite Duras.

The story, another of its author's ventures towards the vanishing points of human personality, relates a brief encounter of two people, between whom only rootless contacts are possible. During the long civic disorder of the Occupation, a young boy has been playing truant from town-life, spending most of his time with another dweller in society's margins, a feeble-minded old lady. Together they play a game; when she wants to sleep, he tells her she's going on a journey and lulls her by imitating the 'sh . . .' of a steam-train. As the Free French follow the retreating Germans into town, the boy brings the old woman a poster, which she is unable to read, proclaiming the liberation. He dresses up in a German soldier's uniform and stands like an eternal sentinel on the Atlantic cliffs. The 'instant of peace' is marked by the sudden cessation of the growling of distant guns; again the waves rustle and winds emptily whine. The liberators take the boy to school, where he improves his reading. The old lady is to be sent to a psychiatric hospital. He visits her for the last time, and repeats a sentence in his reading primer, which dwells on *les rideaux blancs*—the white curtains of bourgeois property-sense, privacy and loneliness.

If this is a minor rather than a major Franju film, it is largely because of an internal imbalance. The wrong sort of emptiness seems to creep into the figure of the old lady, while the boy is played with a sensitivity that is in the end dissatisfying, for one craves a whole feature to trace out the sharp, sad vehemence in his eyes. But the film remains a Franju film, an apparently slight mood-piece which soon leads one to reflections on the very nature of human existence. In this he closely resembles his scenarist, who is, of all *nouveau romanciers*, the nearest to the mainstream. Conversely, the make-believe train-journey is an analogy to the hero's powers of deception in *Thomas l'Imposteur*, to the incantatory nostalgia of *Judex*.

Resnais, suggesting that Riva and her lover possibly stayed together after the film's final title, put on *Hiroshima Mon Amour* a conventionally sentimental interpretation which Marguerite Duras, as its writer, strenuously repudiated. Franju makes any such sentimentality impossible in the case of *Les Rideaux Blancs*, which is as rigorously pessimistic as *Thomas l'Imposteur* would have been without its 'poetic' apotheosis. The almost Beckettian contact of old woman and boy isn't a beautiful

137

friendship, and would jerk no tear from the moistest eye. On his side, it's impatient and superior, on hers, it's mistily inane. At his presentiment of rupture, the boy seems to cling to the friendship, but he's soon reconciled, and is unconscious of any loss. The film underscores the pessimism implicit in the transition in *A Propos d'une Rivière* from young truant to rapacious adult. There is freedom and poetry in these boyhoods, but they remain cul-de-sacs, because only a different society could consolidate the insights they afford.

Instead, it puts the boy behind a desk, where his head is stuffed with notions of happiness quite as arbitrary, and futile, as the steam-train game. From one Occupation to another . . .

The liberation poster contains the same dichotomy: '*Vous êtes libres; engagez-vous.*' After all, if one's rebellions against the values and assumption of a society are sufficiently strong, then one can feel one is living in occupied territory even at home. Though only a Fascist extremist, a nihilist, or a mystic, would seriously maintain that the Liberation was absolutely meaningless, three directors of the Left have used the idea of Liberation ironically. In Autant-Lara's *Le Diable au Corps*, Gérard Philippe walks weeping through the streets while bells and crowds celebrate the 1918 armistice; the woman with whom he was committing adultery was the wife of a sergeant in the trenches. In Clouzot's *Manon*, the Free French soldier frees the pretty little *collaborateuse*, but they have to flee the liberated land together, and die together during another liberation, that of Israel. In Resnais' *Hiroshima Mon Amour*, the Liberation involves the shooting of Riva's lover, the shaving of her hair, her imprisonment by her father, and her heart's entering its state of living death.

For all its shots of Atlantic breakers, of hastily abandoned bunkers, or of moonlit fields, the film never allows that dilatation of the spirit that goes with beauty. The tenuousness of contact is dispiriting, the night-scenes too heavily shadowed to please. This is, in the end, Franju's harshest film, the oppressive style suggesting a total ambivalence as to the meaningfulness, or otherwise, of experience. And the shot of the boy suddenly become a German sentinel, posthumously on guard, has an extremely menacing quality; as if to symbolize another form of spiritual rebellion. Inexplicable as it is, this image is even more disturbing than that of 'the children left behind' at the end of *Hôtel des Invalides*. There one felt them as future victims. This boy stands in for all the executioners to come.

Filmography

SHORTS

1934. LE METRO.
Directed by Georges Franju and Henri Langlois. 16 mm.

1949. LE SANG DES BETES.
Script by Georges Franju. Commentary by Jean Painlevé, spoken by Nicole Ladmiral and Georges Hubert. Photography by Marcel Fradetal. Music by Joseph Kosma (*La Mer* sung by Charles Trenet). Production: Forces et Voix de la France.

1950. EN PASSANT PAR LA LORRAINE.
Script by Georges Franju. Commentary spoken by Georges Hubert. Photography by Marcel Fradetal. Music by Joseph Kosma. Production: Forces et Voix de la France. 31 mins.

1951. HOTEL DES INVALIDES.
Script by Georges Franju. Commentary spoken by Michel Simon and museum guides. Photography by Marcel Fradetal. Music by Maurice Jarre. Production: Forces et Voix de la France.

1952. LE GRAND MELIES.
Script by Georges Franju. Commentary spoken by Madame Marie-Georges Méliès and Lallemant. Photographed by Jacques Mercanton. Music by Georges Van Parys. Art Director: Henri Schmitt. Produced by Fred Orain. Production: Armor Films. 30 mins. With Madame Marie-Georges Méliès and André Méliès.

Note: the version usually seen in England is dubbed with an inexact English commentary.

1953. MONSIEUR ET MADAME CURIE.
Script by Georges Franju, based on *Pierre Curie* by Madame Curie. Commentary spoken by Nicole Stéphane. Photography by Jacques Mercanton. Music: Beethoven (*Les Adieux*). Produced by Fred Orain. Production: Armor Films. 16 mins. With Nicole Stéphane and Lucien Hubert.

1954. LES POUSSIERES.
Script by Georges Franju. Commentary spoken by Georges Hubert. Photography by Jacques Mercanton. Music by Jean Wiener. Produced by Fred Orain. Production: Armor Films. 22 mins.

1954. NAVIGATION MARCHANDE.
Scenario by Rodolphe-Maurice Arlaud. Commentary by Georges Franju, spoken by Roland Lesaffre. Photography by Henri Decaë. Music by Jean-Jacques Grünewald. Production: U.G.C.

1955. A PROPOS D'UNE RIVIERE/LE SAUMON ATLANTIQUE/AU FIL DE LA RIVIERE.
Scenario by Georges Franju. Commentary spoken by Marcel and Jean-Pierre Laporte. Photography by Quinto Albicocco. Music by Henri Crolla. Sound: André Hodeir. Production: Procinex. 25 mins. With Michel Duborgel.

1955. MON CHIEN.
Script by Georges Franju. Commentary by

Jacques Prévert, spoken by Roger Pigault. Photography by Georges Delaunay and Jean Penzer: Music by Henri Crolla. Production: Procinex. 25 mins. With Jacqueline Lemaire.

1956. LE THEATRE NATIONAL POPU-LAIRE.

Script by Georges Franju. Commentary spoken by Marc Cassot. Photography by Marcel Fradetal. Music by Maurice Jarre. Production: Procinex-Antinex. 28 mins.

1956: SUR LE PONT D'AVIGNON.

Script by Georges Franju. Commentary spoken by Claude Dasset. Photography (Franscope, Eastmancolor), Marcel Fradetal. Production: Procinex-Antinex. 11 mins.

1957: NOTRE DAME, CATHEDRALE DE PARIS.

Script by Georges Franju. Commentary by Frédéric de Towarnicki, spoken by Marcel Chaney. Photography (Franscope, Eastmancolor) by Marcel Fradetal. Music by Jean Wiener. Production: Argos-Como. 18 mins.

1958: LA PREMIERE NUIT.

Scenario by Marianne Oswald and Remo Forlani, adapted by Georges Franju. Edited by Henri Colpi. Music by Georges Delerue. Production: Argos. 21 mins. With Pierre Devis and Lisbeth Person.

FEATURES
1958: LA TETE CONTRE LES MURS/THE KEEPERS.

Screenplay by Jean-Pierre Mocky, adapted from the novel by Hervé Bazin. Dialogue by Jean-Charles Pichon. Photography by Eugen

140

Shuftan. Art Director: Louis Le Barbenchon. Edited by Suzanne Sandberg. Music by Maurice Jarre. Sound: René Sarazin. Production Manager: Jean Velter. Production: Atica-Sirius-Elpenor. 98 mins. With Jean-Pierre Mocky (François Gérane), Pierre Brasseur (Dr Valmont), Paul Meurisse (Dr Emery), Anouk Aimée (Stéphanie), Charles Aznavour (Heurtevent), Jean Galland (Maitre Gérane), Edith Scob (a madwoman), Jean Ozenne, Thémy Bourdelle, Rudy Lenoir, Roger Legris, Henri San Juan, Max Montavon.

1959: LES YEUX SANS VISAGE/EYES WITHOUT A FACE/THE HORROR CHAMBER OF DR FAUSTUS.

Screenplay by Jean Redon, from his own novel, adapted by Georges Franju, Jean Redon, Claude Sautet, Pierre Boileau, Thomas Narcejac, with dialogue by Pierre Gascar. Photography by Eugen Shuftan. Special Effects: Assola, Georges Klein. Edited by Gilbert Natot. Art Director: Auguste Capelier. Music by Maurice Jarre. Sound by Antoine Archaimbaud. Produced by Jules Borkon. Production: Champs Elysées-Lux. 90 mins. (in G.B. 88). With Pierre Brasseur (Professor Genessier), Alida Valli (Louise), Edith Scob (Christiane), François Guérin (Jacques), Juliette Mayniel (Edna Gruber), Beatrice Altariba (Paulette), Alexandre Rignault (Inspector Parot), René Génin (Bereaved Father), Claude Brasseur.

The Horror Chamber of Dr Faustus is the title of a dubbed version.

1960: PLEINS FEUX SUR L'ASSASSIN.

Screenplay by Pierre Boileau and Thomas Narcejac, with dialogue by Robert Thomas, Pierre Boileau and Thomas Narcejac. Photography by Marcel Fradetal. Décor by Roger Briaucourt. Edited by Gilbert Natot. Music by Maurice Jarre. Produced by Jules Borken.

Production: Champs-Elysées. 95 mins. With Pierre Brasseur (Count of Kéraudron), Marianne Koch (Edwige), Dany Saval (Micheline), Pascale Audret (Jeanne), Jean-Marie (Jean-Louis Trintignant), Benoist-Sanval (Charles Rollin), André (Philippe Leroy-Beaulieu), Henn (Gérard Buhr), Marthe (Maryse Martin), Serge Marquand, Lucien Raimbourg, Robert Vattier, Jean Ozenne, Georges Bever, Georges Pierre.

1962: THERESE DESQUEYROUX.

Screenplay by François Mauriac, Claude Mauriac and Georges Franju, from the novel by François Mauriac, with dialogue by François Mauriac. Photography by Christian Matras. Edited by Gilbert Natot. Art Director, Jacques Chalvet. Music by Maurice Jarre. Sound by Jacques Labussière. Production Manager, Robert Vignon. Produced by Eugène Lepicier. Production: Filmel. 109 mins. (107 in G.B.). With Emmanuele Riva (Thérèse), Philippe Noiret (Bernard), Edith Scob (Anne de la Trave), Sami Frey (Jean Azevedo), Jeanne Perez (Balionte), Renée Devillers (Mme Victor de la Trave), Richard Saint-Bris (Hector de la Trave), Lucien Nat (Jérome Larroque), Hélène Dieudonne (Aunt Clara), Jacques Monod (Duros), Jean-Jacques Rémy (Specialist).

1963: JUDEX.

Screenplay by Jacques Champreux and Francis Lacassin, based on the original film by Arthur Bernède and Louis Feuillade. Photography by Marcel Fradetal. Edited by Gilbert Natot. Art Director, Gilbert Natot. Music by Maurice Jarre. Costumes by Christiane Courcelles. Sound by Jean Labussière. Production Manager, Jean Maumy. Production: Comptoir Français du Film (Paris)/Filmes (Rome). 95 mins. With Channing Pollock (Judex alias Vallière), Francine Bergé (Diane Monti, alias Marie Verdier), Edith Scob (Jacqueline), Michel Vitold (Favraux), Jacques Jouanneau (Cocantin), Sylvia Koscina (Daisy), Théo Sarapo (Morales), Benjamin Boda (Réglisse), Philippe Mareuil (Amaury de la Rochefontaine), René Génin (Pierre Kerjean), Jean Degrave (The Notary), Luigi Cortese (Pierrot), Roger Gradet (Leon), Ketty France (Jeanne-Marie Bontemps), Suzanne Gossen (Landlady), André Méliès (The Doctor).

1964: THOMAS L'IMPOSTEUR/THOMAS THE IMPOSTER.

Screenplay by Jean Cocteau, Michel Worms, Georges Franju, based on the novel by Jean Cocteau, with dialogue by Jean Cocteau and Raphael Cluzel. Photography by Marcel Fradetal. Edited by Gilbert Natot. Art Direction, Claude Pignot. Music by Georges Auric. Art Direction by Jacques Metehen. Sound by André Hervé, Raymond Gaugier. Production Manager: Georges Casati. Produced by Eugène Lepicier. Production: Filmel. 93 mins. With Emmanuele Riva (Princesse de Bormes), Fabrice Rouleau (Guillaume, alias Thomas), Jean Servais (Pesquel-Duport), Sophie Dares (Henriette), Michel Vitold (Dr Vernes), Rosy Varte (Mme Valiche), Bernard Lavalette (Dr Gentil), H. Dieudonne (Guillaume's Aunt), J. R. Caussimon (The Bishop), André Méliès (Elderly Man at the Ball), Edith Scob (Nurse), Edouard Dermithe (Captain Roy), Gabrielle (Fortune-Teller).

1965: LES RIDEAUX BLANCS (Episode for a planned TV feature L'INSTANT DE LA PAIX).

Script and dialogue: Marguerite Duras. Photography by Marcel Fradetal. Edited by Geneviève Winding. Music by · Georges Delerue. Production: Régie Française de Cinéma with Hélène Dieudonne (the old woman) and Michel Robert (the boy).

PROJECTS

DOCUMENTARIES:
Les Egouts de Paris.
La Salpêtrière.
Le Kremlin-Bicêtre.
L'Académie Française.
Le Miroir des Sports.
Les Halles de Paris.
Les Conditions de Vie des Algériens à Paris.

Franju offered his producers, as an alternative to *Le Sang des Bêtes*, a film about the child sweeps still leading a Dickensian life in Savoy. He refused to make a film saying that pylons spoil the countryside, because he likes pylons.

FROM NOVELS BY EMILE ZOLA:
La Faute de l'Abbé Mouret. Screenplay by Jacques Prévert. With Pierre Brasseur, Brigitte Bardot.
La Terre.
Germinal.

FROM STORIES BY KAFKA:
La Galerie.
La Métamorphose. 'Only for the animal, it would need a real animal. You could never do it with effects . . . Kafka becomes terrifying from the moment that it's documentary.' (But Franju was delighted by Kurt Neumann's film of *The Fly*.)
Le Château, with Jean-Louis Barrault.

OTHER PROJECTS:
Fantomas.
Le Désert des Tartares by Dino Buzzatti.
Du Mouron pour les petits oiseaux, with Monica Vitti.

La Sainte Barthélemy, 'a very expensive production, a sort of social Western. . . . Everyone gets his share of the blame, but since everyone shares the responsibilities and the penalties, it won't annoy anyone; everyone will only see the blame the others get. . . .'

Bijou, from the story by Gyp. 'It couldn't be made because the end isn't moral. They wanted the girl to be punished. But I don't see why she should be punished. She's young, fresh, lucid, cruel, reserved and cynical, a little monster of charm, a jewel. From the moment there's punishment and morality, the fun is ended. But when there's a bad girl the public likes her to be punished. It's one producer's theory that holds good, unfortunately.'

Mademoiselle by Jean Genet. 'If I'd agreed to do *Mademoiselle* with Romy Schneider, I could have made it straight away. But I preferred Emmanuele Riva. Anouk Aimée talked to me about *Mademoiselle* while we were making *La Tête contre les Murs*, because Jean Genet had written it for her. When I mentioned Anouk, the producers replied,"It's not Anouk these days, it's Marie Laforêt." . . . Then one day they said, "Jean Genet would like you to make the film because he liked *Le Sang des Bêtes* so much." I introduced him to Riva. He was very attracted, very moved, he said, by her beauty. He wouldn't hear a word about Romy Schneider: "You've shown me a jewel, I won't swop it against a false pearl, and German at that." Really, but I understood this too late, Genet didn't care who acted in it; he was concerned about something different altogether, and I don't even think it was money. He kept vowing he'd back me up, but didn't he once say, "Who can one betray, if not one's friends?" '

Ben Barka was kidnapped outside the Brasserie Lipp, while going to dine with Franju to discuss a possible film based on his life.

Bibliography

A. TEXTS BY FRANJU

FRANJU, Georges, *Le Style de Fritz Lang*, in *Cahiers du Cinéma* No. 101, November 1959, reprinted from *CINEMAtographe* No. 2, March 1937.

FRANJU, Georges, *Réalisme et Surréalisme*, in KOVACS, Yves, ed., *Etudes Cinématographiques* Nos. 41–42, 1965.

FRANJU, Georges, and PAINLEVE, Jean, *Le Sang des Bêtes* (screenplay), in *L'Avant-Scène du Cinéma* No. 41.

FRANJU, Georges, *Hôtel des Invalides* (screenplay), in *L'Avant-Scène du Cinéma* No. 38.

B. INTERVIEWS WITH FRANJU AND COLLABORATORS

BELLOUR, Raymond, and LACASSIN, Francis, *Pleins Feux sur Pierre Boileau, Thomas Narcejac, Georges Franju et Leur Dernier Assassin* in *Cinéma* 61 No. 54, March 1961.

BUACHE, Freddy, *Entretien avec Georges Franju* in *Positif* 25–26, September 1957.

CAEN, Michel, and ROMER, Jean-Claude, *Entretien avec Jean-Pierre Mocky* in *Midi-Minuit Fantastique* No. 17, June 1967.

CIMENT, Michel, GAUTEUR, Claude,

HAUDIQUET, Philippe, *Entretien avec Georges Franju* in *Image et Son* No. 192, March 1966.

COHN, Bernard, *Franjudex: Entretien avec Georges Franju et Marcel Champreux* in *Positif* No. 56, November 1963.

FIESCHI, Jean-Louis and LABARTHE, André-S, *Nouvel Entretien avec Georges Franju* in *Cahiers du Cinéma* No. 149, November 1963.

LEBOUITS, Jean-Marc and TRANCHANT, Francis, *Entretien avec Georges Franju, Cinéaste et Poète du Merveilleux Quotidien* in *Cinéma* 59 No. 34, March 1959.

TRUFFAUT, Francis, *Entretien avec Georges Franju* in *Cahiers du Cinéma* No. 101, November 1959.

C. ABOUT GEORGES FRANJU: SPECIAL ISSUES OF PERIODICALS

BUACHE, Freddy, *Georges Franju* (monograph), *Premier Plan* No. 1.

VIALLE, Gabriel, GAUTEUR, Claude, CIMENT, Michel and HAUDIQUET, Philippe, *Georges Franju* in *Image et Scn* No. 192, March 1966.

D. ABOUT GEORGES FRANJU: BOOKS

AGEL, Henri, *Miroirs de l'Insolite dans le Cinéma Francais*, Editions du Cerf, 1957.

BORDE, Raymond, and CURTELIN, Jean, in *Nouvelle Vague*, CHARDERE, Bernard, ed., Premier Plan-Serdoc.

KAEL, Pauline, *I Lost it at the Movies*, Little Brown, 1965, Jonathan Cape, & Bantam Books, 1966.

LOVELL, Alan, *Anarchist Cinema*, British Film Institute & *Peace News*, 1962.

E. ABOUT GEORGES FRANJU: MAGAZINE ARTICLES

BENAYOUN, Robert, *Les Festivals: Venise, Zurlini, Toto et Corman di Notte* in *Positif* No. 48, October 1962.

BEYLIE, Claude, *Les Paradoxes de la Fidélité* in *Cahiers du Cinéma* No. 139, January 1963.

BEYLIE, Claude, *Judex ou la Danse des Spectres* in *Midi-Minuit Fantastique* No. 9, July 1964.

BORDE, Raymond, *Pari sur Thérèse Desqueyroux* in *Positif* No. 47, July 1962.

CAMERON, Ian, *Eyes Without a Face* in *Film* 26, 1961.

CAMERON, Ian, *Judex* in *Movie* No. 14, Autumn 1965.

COCTEAU, Jean, *Sur Le Sang des Bêtes* in *Cahiers du Cinéma* No. 149, November 1963.

COWIE, *Franju, Georges*, in *Motion* No. 4 February 1963.

DEMEURE, Jacques, and KYROU, Ado, *Le Plus Grand Cinéaste Francais* in *Positif* No. 16, May 1956.

DOUCHET, Jean, *Venise 1962* in *Cahiers du Cinéma* No. 136, October 1962.

GARRIGOU-LAGRANGE, Madeleine, *Thérèse Desqueyroux* in *Télé-Ciné* No. 108, December 1962-January 1963.

GAUTEUR, Claude, *Franju et la Critique* in *Image et Son* No. 192, March 1966.

GODARD, Jean-Luc, *Georges Franju* in *Cahiers du Cinéma* No. 90, December 1958.

LACASSIN, Francis, *Pleins Feux sur l' Assassin* in *Cinéma* 61 No. 57, June 1961.

LACASSIN, Francis, *De Judex à Judex* in *Cinéma* 64, No. 84, March 1964.

OMS, Marcel, *Plaidoyer pour Thérèse Desqueyroux* in *Positif* No. 53, June 1963.

TAILLEUR, Roger, *Pour un Portrait* in *Présence du Cinéma* No. 1, June 1960.

VIALLE, Gabriel, *A Propos de Georges Franju* in *Image et Son* No. 192, March 1966.

WHITEHEAD, Peter, *Thomas the Imposter*, in *Films and Filming*, May 1966.

F. GENERAL REFERENCES

COOPER, David, *Violence and Psychiatry* in *Peace News* No. 1612.

GARDNER, John, *Whitecoat Conspiracy* in *Peace News* No. 1612, 19 May.

GERRARD, Frank, *Meat Technology*, Leonard Hill, 1964.

GOTTLIEB, Stephen, *Some New Criticism* in *Film Culture* No. 41, Summer 1966.

HAWKS, Howard, cited in BOGDANO-VICH, Peter, *The Cinema of Howard Hawks*, Film Library, Metropolitan Museum of Modern Art, 1962 (and also as *Interview* in *Movie* No. 5, December 1962).

KRIM, Seymour, *The Insanity Bit*, in ROSEN-BERG, Bernard, GERVER, Israel, and HOW-TON, F. William, eds., *Mass Society in Crisis: Social Problems and Social Pathology*, Macmillan, N.Y., and Collier-Macmillan, London, 1964.

ROBBE-GRILLET, Alain, *Old 'Values' and the New Novel* (*Nature, Humanism, Tragedy*) in *Evergreen Review* No. 9, Summer 1959.

ROBBE-GRILLET, Alain, *From Realism to Reality* in *Evergreen Review* No. 39, February 1966.

TAYLOR, Gordon Rattray, *Sex in History*, Thames & Hudson, 1953.